God's Existence Makes Absolutely No Sense. That is Why I Believe.

My Journey
from Tepid Faith Practices to Total
Immersion in God's Infinite Love

James F. Malerba

BookLocker
Trenton, Georgia

Print ISBN: 978-1-958878-21-7
Ebook ISBN: 979-8-88531-381-0

Published by BookLocker.com, Inc., Trenton, Georgia.

Printed on acid-free paper.

BookLocker.com, Inc.
2023

First Edition

Library of Congress Cataloguing in Publication Data
Malerba, James F.
God's Existence Makes Absolutely No Sense. That is Why I Believe. by James F. Malerba
Library of Congress Control Number: 2022921817

"For those who believe, no explanation is necessary. For those who do not believe, no explanation is possible"

(anonymous)

To Matt Becker, with my gratitude and deepest thanks for all the great help you provide for me. Bless you!

Jim Maler

Dedication

I am honored to dedicate this work to the late Father Aidan Kavanagh, O.S.B., my professor, mentor and spiritual advisor at the Yale University Divinity School. He was a brilliant Scripture scholar whose profound knowledge of the gospels, Sacraments, and an inestimable love of God inspired all his students and others whose lives he touched. Without the incredible amount of wisdom and knowledge he imparted to us, I could never have written this book. He was the greatest.

Table of Contents

Introduction

Sometimes in life, things make no sense – wars, hatred, serious illnesses, people who die young, ethnic discrimination, and the like. That said, if those make no sense, then God's existence makes even less sense, about zero, in my mind. Because of that, I believe in him.

This work is a reflection of my journey from an innocent (regarding faith) child to doubting Church teaching to ultimately embracing a total commitment to Jesus, the Sacraments and God's Holy will. I begin with the premise, stated in the title above, that God's existence indeed makes no sense whatever. Such a thought, which I have held for years, laid the groundwork for this journey, which I continue to make every day. Perhaps the following two quotes from *The Five Ways by Saint Thomas Aquinas in proving God's* existence will help you understand what I have written and why they are forever engraved in my heart and soul.

"The Fifth Way is taken from the way in which nature is governed. (1) For we observe that certain things which lack knowledge, such as natural bodies, work for an End. This is obvious, because they always, or at any rate very frequently, operate in the same way so as to attain the best possible result. (2) Hence it is clear that they do not arrive at their goal by chance, but by purpose. (3) But those things which have no knowledge do not move towards a goal unless they are guided by someone or something which does possess knowledge and intelligence-e.g., an arrow by an archer. Therefore, there does exist something which possesses intelligence by which all natural things are directed to their goal; and this we call God."

Let me see if I understand what Aquinas was trying to prove – God has always existed and always will exist. You mean He won't ever die? C'mon – we all die. Right? And I have been taught, by religion teachers, priests and others, that God is one God, but He is actually also three Persons. So, does that not make him three Gods? And more, we learn that He sent His Son to become human through a virgin and get killed and live again? Really? You expect me to believe all that?

I do, and then some.

In each of his Five Ways, Aquinas' arguments provide an indisputable case proving there is an eternal "force" who created everything, from the vast universe to human existence. If God made sense, he would not be God at all, just another flawed being. God is an eternal mystery, and while my Catholic Faith calls Father, Son and Holy Spirit Persons, they are eternal beings, scarcely human, Jesus excepted.

I firmly believe that many doubt God for the simple reason that we all (myself included) see him as an impossible figure. How could someone always exist? Things all have a beginning and end, do they not? Well, that is why we have to reorient our thought processes when it comes to God and believing in Him. We go by the rules of life. God alone goes by other, infinitely conceived rules, and He answers to no one. Admittedly, that can lead a skeptic to pooh-pooh the very thought that there is a higher power and an afterlife.

Recently, I read a statement by the late Stephen Hawking regarding God's existence. Hawking was one of the most brilliant persons of our age, a theoretical physicist whose writings and knowledge were off the charts. Yet, He totally dismissed God, saying,

"We are each free to believe what we want and it is my view that the simplest explanation is there is no God. No one created the universe and no one directs our fate. This leads me to a profound realisation [sic]*. There is probably no heaven, and no afterlife either. We have this one life to appreciate the grand design of the universe, and for that, I am extremely grateful."* (cited from libquotes.com/stephen-hawking/quote)

A wiser and more reasoned viewpoint is this one:

"Truth sees God, and wisdom contemplates God, and from these two comes a third, a holy and wonderful delight in God, who is love." –St. Juliana of Norwich

If nothing else, Hawking's statement was to the point. He certainly did not mince words. In fact, he left no room for rebuttal. No God, no heaven, just a total shutdown of the body and nothing beyond. That statement, however, was a surrender to nothingness – a never-ending black void, if you will – and far beyond pessimistic to the lack of even the possibility there is a loving and forgiving God.

I heard a similar statement when I was an undergraduate at the University of Bridgeport in Connecticut way back in the late 1950s. (Yes, I am an old geezer!) A classmate, majoring in Engineering, took a puff on his cigarette during a discussion on God's existence and said, "How can I, a scientist, believe in God?" First of all, engineers, while in a wonderful profession, are not scientists. Second, his statement held no water. A student's chosen future profession has nothing to do with religion. A few years later, many of my coworkers at the electric company were engineers, and all were faith practitioners in their church or synagogue.

The belief, or lack of it, comes from within, not from without. Yes, people have abandoned their faith for various reasons, which I will discuss as we move through this work. But ultimately it is what is in our hearts that determines whether we choose to believe in God or not. Belief is always intrinsic; outside influences are always extrinsic, though they can certainly influence someone, especially if they are on the fence when it comes to accepting God.

Did I ever doubt God's existence? No, but in college I became lazy about church attendance and almost told my best friend – who later became a priest – that I was considering leaving the Church. How dramatic of me! How collegiate of me, as I listened to fellow students who bragged about their non-faith. Looking back, I should have argued forcefully with them regarding God's existence and his love for all, but my late teenage mindset was also in the doubting phase which was "chic" on college campuses, so I just remained silent.

I never did stop having God or church in my life, but neither did I wear a halo that would blind others. It was an up-and-down path for many years. In the long run, the Holy Spirit put me on the right track. I still feel I am not even close to resembling a saint, but I am trying. I guess that is all God expects of us.

Staying the course on Earth has rewards from God in Paradise that no human mind can ever comprehend. Saint Paul said it so beautifully in his second letter to his co-apostle, Timothy (4:6):

"For I am already being poured out like a libation, and the time of my departure is at hand. I have fought the good fight, I have finished the race, I have kept the faith. From now on there is laid up for me the crown of righteousness, which the Lord, the righteous Judge, will award to me on that day—and not only to me, but to all who crave His appearing."

As I will demonstrate in this work, faith is not only a gift, but also the tremendous realization that we must, if we are to continue to grow spiritually, completely surrender ourselves to God's will. Faith is a journey, sometimes a difficult one, but at the same time wondrous in the peace and love in which it envelops us.

Here is a brief quote from Jean-Pierre deCaussade, a French Jesuit priest who lived in the 17th century. His work, "The Sacrament of the Present Moment," is replete with the wonders of faith and how we become closer to God through our daily practices. In his writings, which Kitty Muggeridge (the wife of Malcom Muggeridge, a British journalist) translated from French to English and published the book "The Sacrament of the Moment," Father deCaussade presented many memorable thoughts. Here are two samples:

"The sacrament of the present moment requires us to do our duty whatever it might be, a carrying out of God's purpose for us, not only on this day, or this hour, but this minute, this very minute – now. This is the way we can all strive for spiritual perfection insofar as it is available in this life." (preface)

"The present moment holds infinite riches beyond your wildest dreams, but you will only enjoy them to the extent of your faith and love. The more a soul loves, the more it longs, [and] the more it hopes, the more it finds." (page 52)

No one is perfect; we are all laden with faults, we commit sins, and many even lose their faith for one reason or another. People can dismiss the very existence of a loving God, but Father de Caussade's words lead us above all the negatives all humans possess, saying perfect faith is eminently available, if we embrace it. Once we unite ourselves completely and forever to God through faith, hope and charity, we are then recipients of that unblemished and flawless faith.

I make no claim to perfection in any way, including faith. Sometimes, even at Mass, I find my mind wandering to other matters, losing focus for a time, even though knowing in my heart I should concentrate on nothing but on the beauty and reality that Jesus is about to come down from heaven as the priest says the words of Consecration.

Yes, I have faith, I have hope, and I try to be charitable in how I treat everyone and give donations, clothes and offer special prayers to poor people and those experiencing tragic or other serious events. But that does not make me perfect. Only a compete surrender to God accomplishes that.

The road to heaven is not easy, but it is doable if we empty ourselves of anger, lascivious actions or thoughts, and other matters that lessen our commitment to the God who made us.

Also, we become faith role models to others through works of charity, giving selflessly of or time, giving comfort to less-fortunate people and in so many other great ways. It is possible, perhaps even likely, that people who witness those charitable acts or our prayer practices, and see that we are deeply committed to others in every way, might be moved to do the same, enhancing their own faith in God. If we all did that, world and family peace would reign. I pray for that as part of my daily offering, though I realize I am just a small, sinful and distracted voice, but also comforted, knowing God hears me.

Will world peace ever happen? Perhaps, but first, billions of the world's inhabitants must all answer the Holy Spirit's urging and become strong believers and faith practitioners. Now, as we move into the beautiful bounty of faith in God, I am hopeful that my own example of a life often flawed but more and more focused and committed to a kind, merciful and forgiving God will be an inspiration to the reader.

Chapter 1:
Is God real?

*"Faith is the realization of what is hoped for
and evidence of things not seen."*

(Hebrews 11:1)

According to the First Vatican Council (1869-70), it is a *de fide* (essential to the faith) dogma of the Catholic Church *"that there is one true and living God, creator and lord of heaven and earth, almighty, eternal, immeasurable, incomprehensible, infinite in will, understanding and every perfection."*

Those words, at their core, provide the definitive and undeniable statement that there is a living, loving God. That said, we have free will to believe or not believe in the Creator or in the Holy Trinity, which is the greatest divine mystery of all. There is no way anyone can prove or disprove its existence. In essence, there is no human mind, no matter how brilliant, that can explain the unfathomable truth that there is but one God, though in three Persons. That becomes the first test as to whether we accept the triune nature of God and commit our entire being to him.

Ask any number of churchgoers if they think God is real, and you most likely will receive a quizzical stare or a curt, "Of course" in return. Believers accept God's existence without question and also accept the reality of three Divine Persons who are not only all equal, but also part of one God, not three.

Through an unshakable faith, we worship a God whose very being makes not even an iota of sense, but who always was, is, and always will be. Not believing is perhaps the saddest way of thinking, and a way to not enjoy the great gift of faith that God, through the Holy Spirit, bestows on every person.

Yes, again, faith is not just a belief; it is an incredible gift. Every human being who has ever lived, is now living, or will in the future be living, is offered that wonderful gift through the grace of the Holy Spirit. Suppose someone offered you an invaluable Christmas or birthday gift. Would you refuse it? Assuming the person offering the gift is honest and sincere, of course you would gratefully accept it.

It is difficult to believe that so many people either do not accept faith or fall away from it for various reasons. Unfortunately, the siren call of the world often lures many millions of people to the secular joys that might include drugs, greed, wanton sex, or a desire to ignore God altogether, putting pleasures over faith.

Let me hasten to add there is nothing wrong or sinful about enjoying a good time at a party, wedding, or other licit activity. It is just when the person is consumed by a love of those things, to the exclusion of God, then sinfulness and pushing God aside come into a life and consume it in all the wrong ways.

That attitude has a prominent and stark example in the gospel of Luke (16:19-31). In the parable of Lazarus and the rich man, we see a man of great wealth, drinking and dining sumptuously every day, while giving no heed to the needs of others, most notably totally ignoring Lazarus, the ragged, poor beggar outside his gate. He never lifts a finger to help him or others, and pays the ultimate terrible price of eternal damnation. With no heed to the fact that his wealth would end the moment he died, the rich man caroused within the good life for years. He must have thought the good times would never end and he would live in the lap of luxury forever.

Well, not quite. He died, as did Lazarus, and both went to opposite places – Lazarus to heaven and the rich man to eternal punishment. Let's examine that for a moment. Was the rich man condemned because of his wealth? No, he suffered forever because he simply did not care about others, especially Lazarus.

Jesus did not offer this parable to condemn wealth *per se,* but rather the love of it to the total exclusion of helping others. And is that not an important component of faith? Helping those in need is a work of mercy and, if done without thought of any reward, is one great way to show God how we love Him, by raising the fortunes of others.

I once read an amusing statement that said, "If we are here to help others, why are the others here?" Maybe that is what the rich man in the parable thought. A few decades ago, a Hollywood actress went to Africa and traveled through some of the poorest of the poor places. A reporter asked her when she returned if what she saw moved her to help through financial or other means. She brushed off the question by saying she was too committed to other things in her life to be involved with assistance to others.

Ouch.

At the other end of the spectrum was actor Paul Newman, whose company products are wildly successful in supermarkets and other outlets. Newman never kept a dime of profits from sales, but rather gave every penny to charities around the nation. More than $40 million benefited those in need. He cared.

So, what is the point of this? No, I am not pontificating or being self-righteous; I am simply pointing out that if we not only possess faith, but also are charitable in giving to others, we are fulfilling God's wishes. The key, of course, is selflessness. When we give with no expectation or reward or recognition, we are doing the right thing. Jesus said, in Matthew's gospel (6:2):

"When you give alms, do not blow a trumpet before you as the hypocrites do in the synagogues and in the streets to win the praise of others... But when you give alms, do not let your left hand know what your right hand is doing, so that your almsgiving may be in secret. And your Father, who sees in secret, will repay you."

Returning to the premise of this opening chapter, yes, God is very real and all-loving, all-knowing and all-forgiving. Thus, when we accept the gift of faith, we accept the responsibilities that go with it – helping others, being sinless as possible, being good parents and spouses, and in many other ways. That makes us all shining lights on the hill and concomitantly influences others positively. When we serve God by example, we serve and inspire others, as well.

Chapter 2:
Who, Exactly, is God?

"The Church's belief about God starts with creation. God is Creator of all that exists. (Gen 1:1; Ps 33:8-9; Ps 124:8; Ps 146:5-6) Yet for the Catholic, God is not merely a Divine Craftsman who works with pre-existent eternal matter, but is the source on which all contingent reality, including matter, depends for its existence. (Acts 17:25: Col 1:16-17). Because God is the Source of all contingent reality, and thus not himself a contingent reality, he must by nature be self-existent, meaning he has the attribute of aseity. In short, God exists necessarily. Unlike the universe and everything in it, nothing is required for God to exist. He simply IS."

(from the catholicthing.org)

That citation perhaps says it best, for believe me, if I had the answer to who God is, I would be on every Catholic TV network, signing book copies, and being invited to the Vatican to ascend to the papacy. Good luck with that dream!

That reminds me of a fictitious cardinal named Sicola. He did not want to be head of the Church, because he feared being called Pope Sicola. (Sorry – I could not help myself.)

Back to business. The title of this book probably answers the question best: God's existence indeed makes absolutely no sense.

First, we are told that God is One, yet in three Persons. Okay, so then there are three Gods. Um no, not quite. The Father is head of the Holy Trinity, the Word, Jesus, is His only begotten one, and the Holy Spirit is as much a Person, consubstantial with the Father and Son and proceeding from them.

Got that? Great! Now, explain it to me, because I don't understand that concept either. Let's give ourselves a rather basic chance of understanding the Trinity by pretending to make a cake.

When making that cake, let us assume we have just three ingredients. All are from the supermarket and, of course, purchased separately. We then pour one ingredient into a mixing bowl, followed by the other two, separately. Then, we mix all the ingredients thoroughly and – voila! – one cake batter, yet three separate but equal ingredients.

Yes, each ingredient is in itself a separate item, yet blended together, it and the other two ingredients "implode" into one entity, a cake batter. So it is with God. Father, Son and Holy Spirit are three separate and distinct Persons, yet all "implode" into one almighty and eternal Godhead. They are co-equal, all-powerful, loving, forgiving, and omniscient.

Beyond that unfathomable mystery, each Person is one to whom we pray separately. We ask the Father for His love and forgiveness; we thank Jesus, the Word for His sacrifice on the cross, his Real Presence in the Eucharist, and for His grace, and we ask the Holy Spirit to guide and lead us through she shoals of life, away from sin and toward the ultimate prize of the eternal kingdom. This all comes together in the Nicene Creed, which we recite at Mass every weekend and on holy days:

"I believe in one God, the Father almighty, maker of heaven and earth, of all things visible and invisible.

I believe in one Lord Jesus Christ, the Only Begotten Son of God, born of the Father before all ages. God from God, Light from Light, true God from true God, begotten, not made, consubstantial with the Father; through him all things were made.

For us men and for our salvation he came down from heaven, and by the Holy Spirit was incarnate of the Virgin Mary, and became man.

For our sake he was crucified under Pontius Pilate, he suffered death and was buried, and rose again on the third day in accordance with the Scriptures. He ascended into heaven and is seated at the right hand of the Father. He will come again in glory to judge the living and the dead and his kingdom will have no end.

I believe in the Holy Spirit, the Lord, the giver of life, who proceeds from the Father and the Son, who with the Father and the Son is adored and glorified, who has spoken through the prophets.

I believe in one, holy, catholic and apostolic Church.
I confess one Baptism for the forgiveness of sins
and I look forward to the resurrection of the dead
and the life of the world to come. Amen."

In that one supplication, we express our firm belief that we accept the entire theology of the Church without doubt or question. We believe in the Holy Trinity, yet as three separate Persons, the love of the Father as Creator of everything, the horrible sacrifice of the Savior in the cross, his glorious resurrection, and the power of the Holy Spirit, who speaks to us as He has spoken through the prophets of old. Further, we acknowledge the role of the church as a catholic, or worldwide entity, and finally we state we believe in the afterlife in the glory of heaven.

It is easy to recite the Creed weekly without giving much thought to its true meaning. A more efficacious way is to read it separately, outside of Mass, and try for a better and deeper understanding of the powerful messages this prayer contains. Embrace every word and phrase, and you will come away with a renewed and enhanced understanding of God's love, mercy, and forgiveness.

The Creed also anchors the nature of God, far better than any other type or form of explanation. God does not just love; God IS love. God does not just forgive; He IS forgiveness. The bottom line is that God's love and desire for all human beings to be saved for the eternal kingdom is endless.

To further understand God's infinite forgiveness, look no further than the suffering Jesus on the cross. In Luke's gospel (23: 39-43), the Roman soldiers tried to increase his humiliation by crucifying him between two wanton criminals. Indeed, one excoriated Jesus scornfully, telling him to save himself and them. The other (now called Saint Dismas by the Church) took the high road, chastising his fellow criminal by noting they deserved their death sentence because of their misdeeds, then adding, "but this man has done nothing criminal."

He then simply asked Jesus to remember him and save him. He was expressing sorrow for his criminal activities and asking for God's forgiveness. Jesus was more than happy to comply, despite his own excruciating agony, saying, "This day, you will be with me in paradise." Does the depth of God's forgiveness get any more stunning or hopeful than that?

As an aside note, it is not a good idea to consider Dismas' last-minute conversion as something worth emulating. Living it up in a sinful and wanton way throughout life, figuring a last-minute cry to Jesus for forgiveness suffices, is not a good path to follow. We do not know when or even how suddenly God will say, "Your time has come." As the Scouting motto says, "Be prepared." Then, you will be in God's eternal grace without end.

Yes, forgiveness from God is always there, right up to the point of death, but is it not better to lead as sinless a life as possible, helping others in need, and being a good person more the path to follow? Rhetorical question.

We are imperfect beings, often drawn to the sinful temptations of the secular world, but having the spiritual strength to turn instead and asking the Holy Spirit for His guidance and help is vastly better. Sure, we fall; that is part of our flawed nature, but getting up from those missteps and seeking God's forgiveness in the confessional gives Satan a well-deserved boot in a certain part of his anatomy and lets us embrace the Lord more fully.

After all, God is everything good and eternally loving and forgiving.

Chapter 3:
God By the Numbers: #1 Father; #2 Son; #3 Holy Spirit (and also #4 Our Blessed Mother)

According to John Philopon *(565 AD), "nature and person are to be identified, or, in h.is language ousia = hypost*

atis. There are then three persons in God who are three individuals of the Godhead, just as we would speak of three human beings and say there are three individuals of the species man. This, instead of admitting to a numerical unity of the divine nature among the three persons in God, this theory postulates only a specific unity, i.e. one species but not one numerical existence."

With that enlightened statement, let us explore the Persons of the Holy Trinity individually.

#1 – God, Our Eternal Father

We begin with #1 – God the Father. First of all, what does he look like? No one on Earth knows. Even John, the disciple Jesus loved, as John proclaimed to be in the prologue his gospel (1:18): *"No one has ever seen God. The only Son, God, who is at the Father's side, has revealed him."* John made a similar statement in his first letter (4:12): *"No one has ever seen God; but if we love one another, God lives in us and his love is made complete in us."*

Centuries before John was born, the prophet Isaiah weighed in on that same topic, saying in 64:3): *"No ear has ever heard, no eye has ever seen, any God but you, doing such deeds for those who wait for him…"*

Incidentally, if Isaiah's statement sounds familiar, the apostle Saint Paul emphasized the rewards of a well-lived life by citing that same Isaiah passage (1 Corinthians 2:9). Neither he nor John nor Isaiah or anyone else, including Moses and Abraham, could ever say they had literally seen the face of God. The Father spoke especially to Abraham and Moses, but neither made a claim to an actual visual sighting of the Creator.

Even Jesus' disciple, Philip, begged the Lord to see God, when he approached Jesus one day and said, *"Master, show us the Father, and that will be enough for us"* (John 14:8). Well, Jesus did tell the disciples just prior to Philip's plaintive request *that "If you know me, you will also know my Father. From now on you do know him and have seen him"* (John 14:7).

The Lord was not one to tease, especially not the disciples. What he said to Philip in response to the latter's request was a mild rebuke, perhaps a gentle dig for not having sufficient faith. Jesus continued with the reproval by noting he and the Father dwell in each other; they are one and the same (John 14:10-11).

Even Moses, who asked God to show him his face, received an unexpected answer from the Lord, who promised Moses he would see God's beauty, but then cautioned (in Exodus 33:20), *"But my face you cannot see, for no man sees me and still lives."* In the human experience, no one could survive seeing the face of God, for it is far more overwhelming in glory and beauty than anything here on Earth.

That raises the question that if we are saved for heaven because of our good works in this life, won't we then see God as He really is, and will we still survive? The answer is a resounding "Yes!" No more will the mystery exist for that person as what God looks like; he or she will be face-to-face with the Father forever. It surely will be overwhelming, but will not result in disaster, such as blindness caused by God's incredible brightness. Rather, in heaven we will be absorbed into the very being and essence of God without end. It is the ultimate reward and will never be taken away.

I once read in our local daily newspaper an incredible story about a man born blind. I forget how the doctors were able to give him sight, though it was through advances in technology.

One of the reporters who interviewed him after this wonderful cure asked the man what his first wish was upon seeing for the first time. The man responded by saying he wanted to know what people looked like. In our spiritual beliefs, is that not what we ask of God? Great news – that will be the case if we merit heaven. Something more than worthwhile to strive for.

The other aspect of what God's appearance might be is certainly not the depiction by Michaelangelo and other worthy artists who showed God as an old man in a flowing robe. Yes, God is a Person, but not in the human sense. He is a pure spirit enveloping every bit of space in the universe, present in even the tiniest speck of dust or the biggest star. You cannot hide from God or pretend he doesn't see some of the things you do. Our Father is omniscient, omnipotent, and also all-forgiving.

An example of that occurred in the classroom of a Catholic high school in Connecticut, where I taught religion for one year.

One of my students questioned my statement that God sees and knows everything. Trying to justify some very inappropriate behavior (which he admitted to me as part of his doubting my statement), he said, "God does not see all the bad things I do." But he did not buy into my response which was, "Then he doesn't see all the good things you do, either." To coin a cliché, you can't have it both ways.

In retrospect, I should have turned that negative viewpoint he held into a more positive one, letting him know that, despite the fact God does not need us, his love is everlasting and his forgiveness are always there for us. The only lost souls are those who turn from God, squander their lives on lascivious pleasures, and die unrepentant.

We must take great comfort in knowing the heavenly Father loves us intently and wants all to be with him without end. Otherwise, why did He send the Son to live among us, and die a horrible death? The redemptive mission was necessary to open the gate of heaven to all believers and faithful ones. We are all his children.

#2 – Jesus, God-Man – Why Don't All Embrace You?

There is so much in the world that leaves me scratching my head. (No, not cooties!) Maybe I am hopelessly naïve or just think wrongly above the neck, but there are some of the mysteries, to me, that exist in life:

Why are there poverty and homelessness?

Why do people commit crimes?

Why are not all of us worshipping God?

Why are there wars?

Why are so many people power hungry, whether in government, corporate life, or greedily gathering huge amounts of wealth?

Related to that, why do those same billionaires pontificate and lecture us to live simply, while they inhabit huge mansions, own private planes and yachts, and live in an opulent lifestyle?

Why do the higher-ups in government tell us that climate change is killing us, yet they fly around the world in private jets, polluting the air every time they travel?

Most important, why did Jesus die for us, especially given all of the above?

That last question, above all others I ask myself, is the one that wrenches my soul every day of my life. It is yet another underscoring of the title of this book, that God's existence makes no sense.

Yes, why did the Eternal Word, the Son of God, take human form, thus humbling himself, live an almost obscure life, and then let himself be subjected to a most excruciating death, preceded by a horrible scourging, being spat upon by Jewish leaders, and mocked as he hung dying on the infamous cross? Didn't he know, being God, that all this was to befall him? He surely did, but even in our belief in God, that question goes unanswered. Moreover, it makes no sense to any of us.

A priest I knew once said that Christ could have redeemed the world with a sigh, a wave of his hand, or by appearing briefly as The Word, pronouncing forgiveness and paradise for all, and then returning to heaven. Why he did not do so? The Father and Son both knew from all eternity that the end result of being born of a woman was to be an almost total rejection by the Jewish leaders and so many of the people themselves. It is part of the eternal mystery.

One of the best explanations of why our savior performed the act of redemption in the way he did came from the words of Father Charles Arminjon (1824-1885), a priest from the town of Chambéry in the French Alps.

After years as a seminary professor, Father Arminjon became a powerful speaker who drew his audiences toward a better understanding of Christ and love of him. I offer the following excerpt from one of his sermons, "The End of the Present World and the Mysteries of the Future Life," (1881) in which he gave an enlightening perspective of the earthly mission of the Lord, and why he took the way he did to save our souls.

"Jesus Christ could have appeared among us, radiant with joy and encompassed by divine splendor. amidst the glitter and pomp of His sovereign majesty. He deemed it more worth of this glory and more profitable to the salvation of men, to show Himself to them girt with a diadem of thorns, clothed in purple and stained with blood, His face bruised. The gaping grimace of death on His lips, bearing the bloody unction of the nails imprinted on His hands and feet.

"In uniting Himself with suffering, Jesus Christ assuredly did not smooth all its severity and all its pangs; but He removed part of its bitterness, corrected and destroyed its poison. He made the chalice of His blood fruitful. Like the brazen serpent set up by Moses in the desert, He implanted Himself in the center of the

world as an inexhaustible instrument of mercy, life and health. Owing to this transformation, His divine wounds, like fountains ever gushing, remain eternally open to all straying and fallen souls who are eager to escape from their coarse, sensual aspirations, wanting to immerse themselves anew in the joys of sacrifice and the honor of purity."

Those simple, straightforward words are possibly the clearest and most effective way to express the reason why Jesus appeared as he did and meekly submitted to death on a cross. The Savior brought the message of peace, love, and the promise of eternal salvation to all who listened to him.

Citations such as those have been a vital cog in my faith journey, and I would be a lot less enlightened without knowing them. They also make me realize why the Eternal Word humbled himself to take human form and preach by words and example how we must live in this world to obtain God's grace and, ultimately, enjoy eternal life.

I sometimes asked myself, so, why didn't everyone in the world acknowledge the Lord as our salvation after he suffered rejection and death? I then realized, after many mental sessions of wondering and pondering that question with the sudden realization I had been overlooking one important gift God has given every human being when he created us from the beginning of time – free will.

It is true that God loves every one of us with a depth we can never understand, Yet millions, and perhaps even billions of people reject God's existence or stop believing or practicing their faith. God endowed every human past, present and future with free will. It is up to us to make good and bad choices, but it is also comforting to know God's forgiveness is always there for the asking.

No one can deny we make our own choices, but what exactly is free will? A fine and credible answer from Catholic Answers online helps better understand the nature of this great gift from God:

"Catholic teaching on free will recognizes that God has given men and women the capacity to choose good or evil in their lives. The bishops at the Second Vatican Council declared that the human person, endowed with freedom, is 'an outstanding manifestation of the divine image.' (Gaudium et Spes, No. 17) As the parable of the Grand Inquisitor in Dostoevsky's novel, The Brothers Karamazov, makes so beautifully clear, God did not want humanity to be mere automatons, but to have the dignity of freedom, even recognizing that with that freedom comes the cost of many evil choices.

"However, human freedom does not justify bad moral choices, nor does it justify a stance that all moral choices are good if they are free: 'The exercise of freedom does not imply a right to say or do everything.' (The Catechism of the Catholic Church, No. 1740) *Christian belief in human freedom recognizes that we are called but not compelled by God to choose constantly the values of the Gospel—faith, hope, love, mercy, justice, forgiveness, integrity and compassion."*

A more ancient statement regarding God's gift of free will is found in the Book of Sirach (15:11-17):

"Do not say [about God]: 'He himself has led me astray,'" for he has no need of the wicked. Abominable wickedness the

LORD hates, and he does not let it happen to those who fear him. God in the beginning created human beings and made them subject to their own free choice. If you choose, you can keep the commandments; loyalty is doing the will of God. Set before you are fire and water; to whatever you choose, stretch out your hand. Before everyone are life and death, whichever they choose will be given them."

In a more succinct way, we can say, "You made your bed, lie in it." The type of bed can be heavenly or, well, not heavenly.

A lighthearted but apocryphal example of free will choices is this: A man, highly successful in business, died and went to heaven. Saint Peter showed him around and the man was blown away by the beauty of heaven. Saint Peter advised the man he also had to spend one day in hell and then make his eternal choice.

The man took the elevator far down to hell. When the doors opened, he was shocked to see a wonderful golf course, and his old fellow executives rushing to greet him. He golfed, ate delicious meals and drank freely, and then returned to heaven. He told Saint Peter that heaven was wonderful, but hell was much better than he expected.

Down he went again. The doors opened, and suddenly the elevator disappeared. The second trip left the man speechless. Raging fires burned him, screams of agony were everywhere. The man, totally shocked, asked the devil, "What is this all about?" The devil smiled and said, "Yesterday you were a visitor. Today, you're a permanent resident."

The moral is, you make your own choices, good and bad, and the consequences are self-made. Free will is ours, as are our paths to love or something less. Jesus, of course, being God himself, and also fully human, had the same free will. He could have used that will to convince one and all that he was the only path to salvation, but he did not do so. His mission was not to command or demand, but to offer the gift of grace to all who embraced his word. He never interfered with our free will, but rather left the choice of belief or nonbelief strictly up to us.

The Savior's own free will as being fully human as well as being fully Divine did not stop him from being rejected and suffering death. As God, Jesus could have avoided all that comprised his Passion, but that was not at all the way he chose. He had to be rejected and die on the cross, to fulfill the Scriptures, and to effect human redemption.

John's gospel has a number of statements by the Lord relating to our earthly choices that are both hopeful and cautionary. In 8:51, Jesus said to the disbelieving Pharisees, *"Amen, amen, I say to you, whoever keeps my word will never taste death."*

As they usually did, the Pharisees mocked Jesus by asking him if he was greater than Abraham, who died. Jesus, of course, meant eternal death in hell, not an earthly death. He also tried to tell those obtuse Pharisees in John's gospel that he was the way to salvation (10:9):

"I am the gate. Whoever enters through me will be saved, and will come in and go out and find pasture." But you do not believe, *because you are not among my sheep. My sheep hear my voice; I know them and they follow me. I give them eternal life, and they shall never perish"* (10:27-28). The Lord followed up by adding, *"The Father and I are one."* (10:30)

That was the last straw for the Jews, who picked up rocks to stone Jesus. But the real rocks were in their unbelieving heads, where they would rattle right through the crucifixion and beyond.

At no time did Our Savior wave a Divine hand and say, "Poof – you will all now believe in me and be saved." Sure, he could have done just that and spared himself from the cross. Sure, he could have set up a throne and ruled here on Earth until the end of all time. Also, the Father could have removed free will from humanity and replaced it with a forever binding of faith. Think about it, and you will realize that free will is an integral and indispensable part of our human makeup, nothing less. Without it, we would be mere automatons.

We are on Earth for a relatively short time, and then life as we know it ends. It is best, then, to view our existence and gift of life as a trial period, an extended test, if you will, that determines where the road will take us from this life to one that will never end. Believe and enjoy eternal life; do not believe and be condemned.

Those are harsh words, but they are not mine. Jesus preached both hope and despair in regard to believing in him or rejecting him, saying, *"...the hour is coming in which all who are in the tombs will hear his [Jesus'] voice and will come out, those who have done good deeds to the resurrection of life, but those who have done wicked deeds to the resurrection of condemnation."* (John 5: 28-29)

The Lord told that to the Jews following the cure of a crippled man at the pool called Bethsesda on the Sabbath. Because he violated Mosaic law by curing on the Sabbath, and also that he called himself God's Son, the Jews tried to kill him. After all, he

29

blasphemed by saying he was equal to the Father (John 5:16-18). Hardened hearts and closed minds are often difficult to penetrate and to accept the truth. Why do they not listen?

The answer to that question is that there is no logical answer. The reasons as to why the redemptive process went the way it did are left up to us to accept and believe, or reject and not believe. Simple as that. Free will is both a blessing and a curse, depending on the road each of us chooses.

It was a frustrated Jesus who, despite performing so many miracles, still could not win over many of the Jews. After telling them he was the Son of Man and not being believed, he hid himself from them. This was after his greatest miracle, the raising of Lazarus from the dead. The chief priests, rather than admiring and being astonished at bringing Lazarus back to life, decided both he and Jesus had to be killed. The desire for absolute power and control consumed them.

It seems impossible to believe that the cures of blind and crippled people and others would receive such a negative response. This was especially true when Jesus cured on the Sabbath. There were seven such instances (list from Steve Shirley on Jesus alive.cc/miracles-Jesus-performed-on-sabbath)

#1. Cast an unclean spirit out of a man (Mk 1:21-28) (Lk 4:31-37)

#2. He3aled Peter's mother-in-law, who had a fever (Mt 8:14-15) (Mk 1:29-31) (Lk 4:38-39)

#3. Healed the man with the withered hand (Mt 12:9-13) (Mk 3:1-6) (Lk 6:6-11)

#4. (Jn 5:1-18) – Healed the lame man by the pool of Bethesda

#5. (Lk 13:10-17) – Healed the crippled woman

#6. (Lk 14:1-6) – Healed the man with dropsy
#7. (Jn 9:1-7,14) – Healed the man born blind

When Jesus cured the man ill for thirty-eight years on the Sabbath (#4), the Jews began persecuting him for doing what under Mosaic law was forbidden. However, when Jesus cured the woman totally bent over and unable to straighten up, the people who witnessed the miracle cheered the Lord. The synagogue leader who had raised his voice in opposition was humiliated and silenced (Luke 13:11-17). Believers in Jesus shut down the man, who was not a believer.

A slightly different result occurred when Jesus cured the man with dropsy on the Sabbath (#6). The Pharisees and scribes could not answer when the Lord asked if it was or was not lawful to cure on the Sabbath. Once again, the silence was deafening. Finally, cure #7 met with incredulity by the Jewish leaders, triggering a lengthy account of the man cured of his blindness The heart of that account when the Pharisees questioned the man and then his parents. In the end, the Pharisees, angry that the formerly blind man lectured them because of their unbelief, threw him out.

What is the underlying message for all of us in those Sabbath cures? The lesson in all was not just for the Jewish leaders, or the crowds witnessing the miracles. Rather, it was a lesson for every one of us. Jesus was demonstrating to the mostly nonbelieving audience that there was to be no limit to helping others, Sabbath or any other day. When the Jewish leaders interrogated the once-blind man Jesus cured on a Sabbath, and he told them who had performed the miracle, they persecuted the Lord. Jesus, however, as always, had the perfect answer: *"My Father is at work until now, so I am at work"* (John 5:17-18).

Those hard-of-heart men did not believe a word, but instead doubled down on their hatred and incredulity. Not only did this itinerant preacher cure on the Sabbath, but he just made himself equal to God. He blasphemed and must be killed!

As followers of Christ, we acknowledge Jesus as fully human and fully Divine. And we also must understand that curing on the Sabbath was a deliberate act, for the Lord was telling all who would ever live that the New Order began with him.

As a practical example, what would happen to a critically injured or ill person if doctors were not allowed to help them on a Sabbath? Suppose police officers could not stop crimes or make arrests on a Sabbath? If firefighters could not rush to a house or building fire on the Sabbath, how many lives might be lost?

Yes, that is silly and not part of our society's practices, but the ancient Jewish law forbade cures and work, among other things, on the Sabbath day. That said, they were enraged by Jesus' actions not because he cured, but because they could sense they were losing control over the people and could not let that happen.

That same attitude and craving for power and control over the people is mirrored today around the world in many nations, where Draconian laws are passed to suppress freedom and human spirit. Jesus was born not to assume power forever on Earth, but to open the way to heaven for all believers. He signaled the New Age, one that would have no end if we love and believe in him.

There is, of course, the most important act Jesus performed, on the same night he allowed himself to be arrested and suffer incredible beatings and tortures, then being hung on a cross like a common thief or murderer. Yes, the Sabbath and other cures were incredible, but the most meaningful and truly spectacular gift came at the Last Supper.

Before getting to the institution of the Eucharist, put yourself into that upper room with the disciples. The Twelve began the evening, but only eleven remained after Jesus told his betrayer, Judas Iscariot, *"What you are going to do, do quickly."* (John 13:27) No one had even an inkling as to what Jesus meant. Had you been dining with Jesus and the disciples that night, you would also not have had any idea that the God-man was about to leave them and Earth.

What you might have wondered is why Jesus called the meal a Passover feast. It was not yet Passover, but rather Preparation Day. We know this from John's gospel 19:31 because after Jesus died on the cross, the Jews asked that the legs of the two criminals hanging with Jesus be broken, since so they would not remain on their cross on the Sabbath, which that year was also the Passover. It is curious that the gospels do not say whether any of the disciples questioned the Lord as to why he was holding the prescribed Passover meal a day early, though he even told the Twelve they would be celebrating the Passover meal (Matthew 26:18; Mark 14:14; Luke 22:8-9; John 13:1).

If the disciples were puzzled at that point, that is understandable. the Lord had told them to locate a man and tell him they would all celebrate the Passover meal in his home. The disciples did as they were told, perhaps thinking the meal would be held on the actual feast day. They had no idea the Lord was going to have the meal before Nisan 15, traditionally the actual day Passover began (and still does).

This was yet another lesson for the disciples regarding the end of the old way and the beginning of a new one. What Jesus was telling his beloved followers subtly was that the New Passover was about to occur. That immortal event came following the meal, when Jesus blessed bread and gave it to the disciples, telling them, "This is my body." He then took the cup of wine and told them all to drink of it, "for this is the blood of my covenant, which will be shed on behalf of many for the forgiveness of sins" (Matthew 26:28), Mark (14:22-25), Luke (22:19-20), and Saint Paul, First Corinthians (11:23-25).

The greatest gift Jesus gave to all humanity was himself, body and blood, soul and divinity. Everything else in our world pales by far in comparison to the Eucharist.

John is the only gospel writer not to record the Eucharistic pronouncements, but he devoted four chapters (14-17) to Jesus' discourses at that feast. I highly recommend studying the content of those four chapters, because they lay out what Jesus proclaimed to the disciples, giving them a lengthy theological lesson and cementing his Sonship with the Father and also letting the disciples know the Holy Spirit would come to them and give them the courage, knowledge and power to proclaim the Good News. (John 15:26-27)

An unfortunate note here related to the institution of the Eucharist by the Lord: In 2019, a Pew Research survey of people who identified as Catholics reported that of those who participated in the survey, which asked of each participant if he or she believed in the Real Presence of Jesus in the Blessed Sacrament. Incredibly, some sixty-one percent said no, that the Consecration rite is just a symbolic action.

I beg to differ, as so many others do, minority status notwithstanding. If you look back a few paragraphs, you will read that Matthew, Mark, Luke and Paul all used exactly the same language. Jesus did not say, "This bread represents my Body, and this wine represents my Blood." Nor did he say either was symbolic of his Body and Blood. He clearly stated, (emphasis mine), "This IS my body; this IS my blood."

Doubting the Real Presence is scarcely a new phenomenon. I the early years of this century, my parish priest told us, at a parish council meeting, that he was approached by a woman after Mass. He had given a homily on Jesus' presence in the Eucharist clearly and forcefully. He said the woman asked him, "Father, why make such a fuss over a piece of bread?" Needless to say, he was both shocked and dismayed.

Similarly, someone I have known for years and, perhaps ironically, a convert to Catholicism, said exactly the same thing. When I pointed to the Lord's words and said he meant them literally, he told me I was wrong, that it was just a symbol, and he could not ever accept such a thing as the Real Presence.

If the Consecration is just a symbolic and not real act, our Catholic Faith is no different from any other Christian denomination. No, it *is* true. When the priest, ordained and fully in power to consecrate the bread and wine says the same words Jesus gave his disciples, the Lord comes down from heaven and envelops the entire congregation in his love. That we have been chosen to receive that same Body and Blood is the greatest gift and miracle of all.

The bottom line is I am so grateful God gave me the gift of faith and, through the Holy Spirit (more about him shortly) helped me understand the presence of Jesus Christ, called down from heaven at every Mass. It is something that staggers my mind and makes me feel insignificant but also gratified at the same time. I pray as Communion time approaches, that I am receiving Jesus worthily and that he will continue to be with me as I struggle with life's temptations, vagaries and day-to-day challenges. I strongly feel he does.

Dear reader, Jesus IS Really and Truly Present in the Eucharist and just wants us to be in the state of grace, so we can let him come to us worthily. Receive him with joy and with the knowledge you are bringing the Son of God, the Eternal Word, into your own body and soul. Nothing else in the world matters when Jesus is the center of your life.

The Son of God is always the center of my own life, and the Eucharist is the most important food I receive every day. I am so grateful that he, through the guidance of the Holy Spirit, has given me the depth of faith that enables me to lead a better moral and ethical life and may I always receive him worthily.

It is not easy to stay on the straight and narrow in our world. Daily, temptations and other works of Satan and his angels abound. Immorality, sinning in other ways, such as excessive drinking, gambling, being greatly unkind or scornful of others or in so many other ways cause us to diminish our faith and fall victim to the siren call of the "good life." Jesus never said it would be easy. As he cautioned,

"Enter through the narrow gate, for the gate is wide and the road broad that leads to destruction, and those who enter through it are many. How narrow the gate and constricted the road that leads to life. And those who find it are few" (Matthew 7:13-14).

Hope for salvation also came from Old Testament writings. Centuries before Our Lord was born, the Book of Proverbs (24:16) had a passage cautioning that no one is perfect and all are subject to sinning:

"For the just man falls seven times and rises again, but the wicked stumble to ruin."

So, it is a fact of life that we sin, but it is seeking God's forgiveness that helps us to rise again. I will have more on that in the next chapter, on the Sacrament of Penance.

Many years ago, I read an article in which Dick McPherson, then the football coach at Syracuse University, was being interviewed by a reporter. The reporter had heard that McPherson attended Mass every morning and remarked that he must be a saint. McPherson replied honestly, "Young man, my church is for sinners, not for saints."

His sentiment is expressed in a bit more detail that Church is not a meeting place for saints, but rather for who want to lead a richer spiritual life on this site: inallthings.org/is-the-church-for-sinner-or-saints

"...it's a safe haven for sinners. We're in church because we need God, and we need God because we aren't perfect and we can't make ourselves better. Grace is not for the "saved"—it is for those who need a Savior."

I also go to morning Mass every day, but I still have to live in a sinful world and try my best to avoid sin and temptation. It is not easy, and though I like to joke that I go to Mass to get my halo polished, believe me, it would never blind anyone. The Eucharist I receive is my strength against Satan, and when I am tempted it is the Divine Power, especially that of the Holy Spirit, that keeps me focused and my eyes on things beyond this life. I often recall the beautiful words of Saint Paul in Second Timothy (4:7-8):

"I have competed well; I have finished the race; I have kept the faith. From now on the crown of righteousness awaits me, which the Lord, the just judge, will award me on that day, and not only to me, but to all who have longed for his appearance.3"

That statement is so uplifting and gratifying! Paul was scarcely bragging; he certainly did not have a good start when Christianity was in its infancy. Yes, it took Jesus himself to change this to-be saint, but he never hesitated, nor did he ever quit in his quest to bring the Faith to others. He endured stoning, falls, shipwrecks, scourging and imprisonments without ever giving up or abandoning Christ and the Faith. Indeed, the crown for him was more than merited.

For us, that same crown awaits all who denounce Satan and all evil and keep God's word faithfully.

#3 – My Special Pal, the Holy Spirit

"Saint Joseph wants you to be docile to the direction of the Holy Spirit so that you can be led in the ways of holiness. What is holiness anyway? Is it some unfathomable spiritual summit you can never hope to reach? No, it is not. Holiness is living in intimate, loving communion with God. More specifically, holiness is observing the two great commandments of love of God and neighbor, avoiding sin, leading a life of virtue, and abiding in sanctifying grace. None of this is possible without the Holy Spirit in your life." (Father Donald Calloway MIC, a priest of the Fathers of the Immaculate Conception of the Most Blessed Virgin

Mary, Qtd. In The Morning Offering in thecatholicthing.org August 2022)

Okay, so I took a little liberty with the above title. No, the Holy Spirit and I do not meet, share conversations, hoist cold ones, or really pal around together. But we meet every day spiritually, and his voice guides me every waking moment. Further, he has guided me throughout my life, and I will now prove it.

When I was about eleven years old, my mother was visiting my aunt and uncle, who had a walk-up attic in their home. As we all know, attics can be fascinating places where we rummage around old books, trinkets, and other things. Like all other young kids, I loved exploring that space and visited it every time we went to their home. One day, I was walking along the attic floor and became distracted by something that caught my eye. A sudden feeling (not even a voice) made me look down. I had one foot over the edge of the big opening to the staircase. Had I taken another step, these words would never have seen the light of day.

My next example is not as dramatic, but telling, nonetheless. Coming out of daily Mass one morning not long after my wife passed away in 2018, I was getting into my car when a thought struck me vividly. It urged me to write a book on God's presence in nursery rhymes. I said to myself, "Yeah, right" and dismissed the notion immediately.

But the Holy Spirit is persistent, and that same thought started nagging me. I decided to order a book from Amazon containing more than one hundred nursery rhymes and culled about seventy that could be said to have a connection with God. Six months later, my first (self) published book came out: *"God is Everywhere – Even in Nursery Rhymes!"*

I have to say the Holy Spirit was far from letting me relax when it came to writing books. My next effort, also self-published, was "Seeing 'Flower Petals' Reveal Themselves Slowly: A Guide to Understanding and Interpreting the Parables of Jesus." Did that end things, at least for a while? Uh, uh. Just as the Spirit doesn't take time off, neither did he let me do so.

In 2022, my third effort hit the computer I began writing a book designed to bring a deeper spiritual meaning to the reader titled, *"Our Beautiful Catholic Prayers: What Are They Really Saying to Us? Uncovering the Underlying Meanings within Them."* (Still in the formative stagtes.)

My fourth is the one you are now reading. Paradoxically, it was both the easiest and at the same time most difficult for me to write. Personal accounts can be seen by the reader as self-serving, and that was not at all my intent as the Spirit and I worked together to produce these chapters. He gave me the words to write; I only did the typing. My goal was to show readers the wonderful and infinite beauty of our Catholic Faith and how it is our path to heaven.

There was another, though earthly person, who was indirectly involved in spurring me to write books on the Faith. He was another strong inspirational source; his name was Father Aidan Kavanagh, O.S.B., a Benedictine monk, to whom I have dedicated this book. He was my advisor and mentor at the Yale University Divinity School. His brilliant, yet down-to-earth approach to the parables, faith practices and the liturgies were invaluable. My classmates and I all learned volumes from him and have never forgotten the insights he possessed and shared with all his students, colleagues, and faith practitioners. He is in heaven now, probably still mentoring and advising. I hope so.

Enough personal distraction; who is the Holy Spirit and what exactly is his role in our lives? He is the Third Person of the Holy Trinity, all-powerful, all-knowing-all loving, as are the Father and the Son. Yet, we know so little about this Paraclete, even to what his appearance might be.

In Luke 3:22, the Spirit descended on Jesus in the form of a dove, as the Father praised His beloved Son. After Jesus' Resurrection, he promised to send the Holy Spirit, and in Acts 2:2-4, the Spirit came upon the apostles as a driving wind and with tongues of fire for each of them.

From Matthew through Revelation, the Holy Spirit occupies a very prominent place. John the Baptist (in Mark 1:8) proclaimed that while he baptized with water, the One to come would baptize with the Holy Spirit. All told, there are nearly one hundred references to the Paraclete in the New Testament. I commend your attention to the entire list at the end of this work, for it shows how the Old Testament writers, the apostles, Saint Paul and other earliest Christians embraced the Spirit, knowing the intimate role he played in their lives, guiding and leading them always.

Some years ago, a priest wrote, in a newsletter for a Catholic organization, that the Holy Spirit, to some, is the "unknown" Person of the Trinity. Why might that be? One reason is that our Mass and private prayers are almost exclusively devoted to the Father, Son and Blessed Mother. That is not to say we ignore the Spirit; after all, when we make the Sign of the Cross, recite the Creed or say the rosary, the Holy Spirit is an integral presence.

He does get short shrift in the Apostles Creed, where only four words are devoted to him: "with the Holy Spirit." Aha, but he does get more "press" in the Nicene Creed, which is the one most celebrants now ask us to recite at weekend Masses:

"I believe in the Holy Spirit, the Lord, the giver of life, Who proceeds from the Father and the Son, Who with the Father and the Son is adored and glorified, Who has spoken through the prophets."

Now, that lays out the magnificent role the Spirit plays in the human experience. He is consubstantial with the Father and Son, is all-knowing, all-loving, all-powerful, and all-forgiving He is as much adored and glorified as they are, and his influence was one with the Old Testament prophets.

The greatest example to me as to the Spirit's presence in the writings of the prophets is in the four servant oracles in the Book of Isaiah. Each oracle is unmistakably referring to Jesus. The first (42:1-9) describes what the Messiah will do when he comes. The second (49:1-7) promises to make the servant the light to all nations, yet he will be despised and abhorred. In the third (52:13-15) Isaiah makes a vague reference to the crucifixion of the Messiah, saying the servant will be raised high and exalted. That oracle also warns the servant will be so marred by torture as to be unrecognizable.

In the fourth Servant Oracle (53:1-12), we encounter an uncanny and almost frightening in its accuracy an account of the Messiah's (Jesus') passion and death. In the previous oracle, the prophet mentioned the trials the servant would undergo. But in the fourth oracle, what Isaiah wrote is graphically on the mark, making a dire prediction depicting almost exactly what happened to Jesus when he was scourged and then hung on the cross.

The prophet had no way of knowing that, almost seven centuries later, the Messiah would be born, embark on his mission to preach his messages of love, warning, and promise, and then be put to death, which makes Isaiah's writing not of his own but that under the influence of the Holy Spirit.

I highly recommend that you read the four oracles and see the progression from introducing the servant in the first oracle to the suffering servant in the fourth oracle. I think you will be deeply touched and possibly made uncomfortable by the final oracle, but absorbing all the four oracles will enhance your understanding of the Holy Spirit's way of being with us, whether we are prophets or just everyday people of faith. He loves us all and gently nudges to the kingdom of heaven by encouraging more and meaningful faith practices.

Every morning, as part of my daily prayers, I ask the Holy Spirit to guide my way, keep me from sinning, and help others in need. With him in my life, for all he has done for me over the many years, I am eternally grateful. I hope I am deemed worthy of heaven when I leave this life, and I want to embrace the Holy Spirit and thank him for all his wonderful help. My existence would not have been so fulfilling without him.

#4 – Adoring and Praising Our Blessed Mother

Mary, the humble virgin who was to become the greatest woman ever to walk the face of the earth, came into my life early on, probably at the same time I began my preparation classes for Confession and First Holy Communion. (More about that process later.) I knew little about her at such a young age, even though I saw her statue at our church every week.

A greater awareness of Mary as our Blessed Mother came to me gradually, not in a sudden blinding flash of revelation. I thank her daily for her intercessions and for inviting me to pray to her. It is such a great honor to offer supplications to the woman who bore the Son of God and who was born, lived and died sinless. No other human being who ever lived, other than Jesus himself, is worthy of her magnificence.

Ditto for the rosary. We youngsters were all taught the Hail Mary, but nothing beyond that, except to have the nuns who visited our parish weekly for religious instruction fill our developing minds by emphasizing the miracle of Mary being conceived without sin. Of course, who knew what that even meant? Seven-year-olds are not yet able to process concepts, and I was no exception. All I and the others my age knew was she was somebody really special. Boy – were our eyes opened a few years later, when we discovered all Mary was, and is!

I think it was around the time I began my next preparation with my friends and classmates for Confirmation that I became familiar with the rosary. Please excuse some of the guessing, but so much time has passed since then that exact dates or years are long forgotten. (For you younger people reading this book, see what you have to look forward to?)

Conversely, so-called senior moments have their advantages. In old age, forgetting exact dates, places and even people are excused by younger people, who indulge our memory lapses. At least, I hope they do!

For me, reciting the rosary became an occasional prayer; it was not until college days rolled around that I said the beads daily, and then only during Lent. Today, the rosary is in my hands before Mass every morning, when our little group gathers daily to recite the mysteries of a given day. I participate by reciting the fourth decade. Sometimes I also recite it privately, as a supplication for a family member or friend who needs special prayers.

The Blessed Mother has been a kind of partner in prayer for me for many years, and that will never change. She means everything to me.

That said, our Blessed Mother's role is often misunderstood, especially by non-Catholics and non-Christians. I still vividly remember a classmate at the University of Bridgeport back in the 1950s, who made snide remarks about Our Lady. He was much older than the rest of us, probably in his 40s, and was a minister, to boot.

One day, while I was in between classes, I was reading in the lounge of a classroom building, and he was sitting nearby. Without any preliminaries – not even greeting me as I sat down – he muttered, *sotto voce* – " Mother-worshipping church" and a few other things I did not catch. He definitely was not wishing any Catholic a happy birthday.

Perhaps I should have answered him in a stronger way, but instead I just politely told him we Catholics do not worship Mary, just God. The Blessed Mother is to be a direct object of prayers and supplications and is to be adored and admired, but never, never worshipped. He did not answer, so I was not sure if I got through to him.

That minister's statement is one I have heard from others. I believe part of the reason is that the Church has such a deep devotion to Mary. And why not? She was the only person after Adam and Eve, to be born without the stain of original sin. She was the only one ever visited by an angel to proclaim to her the incredible role she was to have in her life. Mary, the sinless, devout young Jewish girl, was to become forever the Mother of God.

Think about that astounding gift the angel Gabriel announced that was being imparted by God to her. MOTHER OF GOD! Scoffers might well say God did not need a Mother; he was his own person, not in need of a mother. Enter Jesus Christ nine months later. The Son and the Mother were destined to bring salvation to the world. She was the mother of the Redeemer.

Not a day goes by, especially when I recite the Hail Mary as I say the rosary or in other spiritual exercises, that I am not awestruck by these three words: "Mother of God". Frankly, they blow my mind away every time I say them. The frightened young Jewish girl, startled by an angel, was to become forever the object of love and admiration. She is called the co-redemptrix by the Church and is that, and much more. She hears and answers our prayers directed to her. Little wonder we venerate, but never worship her.

Besides the Holy Trinity, she is above all angels and saints in heaven. Yet, when she has made her earthly appearances, she has appeared almost exclusively to people of lesser means, not to members of the elite class. My first example, which follows, demonstrates this vividly.

(Author's note: The following is reproduced from an article by Francesco Merlo in vaticannews.va/en/church/news/2018.)

"Mary's first earthly appearance, in which she called herself the Mother of God, Our Lady and the mother of all humanity, was in 1531, when she appeared on the hill of Tepeyac in Mexico to an indigenous peasant, Juan Diego. He saw a glowing figure on the hill. After she had identified herself to him, Our Lady asked that Juan build her a shrine in that same spot, in order for her to show and share her love and compassion with all those who believe.

"Afterwards, Juan Diego visited Juan de Zumárraga, who was Archbishop of what is now Mexico City. Zumárraga dismissed him in disbelief and challenged the future Saint to provide proof of his story and proof of the Lady's identity. Juan Diego returned to the hill and encountered Our Lady, who told him to climb a hill and pick the flowers he was to find.

"Although it was winter and nothing should have been in bloom, Juan Diego found an abundance of flowers of a type he had never seen before. The Virgin bundled the flowers into Juan's cloak, known as a tilma. When Juan Diego presented the tilma of exotic flowers to Zumárraga, the flowers fell out and he recognized them as Castilian roses, which are not found in Mexico. What was even more significant, however, was that the tilma had been miraculously imprinted with a colorful image of the Virgin herself.

"This actual tilma, preserved since that date and showing the familiar image of the Virgin Mary with her head bowed and hands together in prayer, represents the Virgin of Guadalupe. It remains perhaps the most sacred object in all of Mexico."

Perhaps the most well-known of all of the Blessed Mother's apparitions occurred in the year 1858 to a peasant French girl, Marie-Bernarde Soubirous (now Saint Bernadette). Mary appeared to her 18 times at Lourdes in France and who, when Bernadette asked who she was, said, *"I am the Immaculate Conception."* When Bernadette reported this to her parish priest, he was astounded, for the doctrine of Mary's Immaculate Conception eight years earlier was not widely known at that time. Since the apparitions, Lourdes has been the site of many healings and other miracles, and is visited by countless numbers of pilgrims each year.

In Fatima, Portugal, Our Lady came to three young children and warned them what was to happen in Russia, which would become a world power and spread its God-hating influence over so much of Eastern Europe. She imparted three secrets to the children, two of which have been revealed, but not the third one, except partially. We are left to our vivid imaginations as to what it said.

Those three are but a few of the appearances Our Blessed Mother has made to people. One consistent thread is that all to whom she spoke were indigent or of lesser means than others in their towns. Jesus, cited in Matthew (5:3), said when he gave his audience the Beatitudes, *"Blessed are the poor in spirit, for theirs is the kingdom of heaven."* The Lord had a special affinity for the poor, knowing they were struggling, yet keeping and growing in their faith without any reservations.

Remember, Jesus did not come flying down to Earth on a golden chariot, nor did he live in a mansion. Throughout his entire ministry, he was humble, cautioned against the love of money, and set down the Pharisees and other arrogant types. Many times, he has sent Mary to us with messages of hope and warning, sometimes both in the same appearance. Beneath all that is his unending love for every person in the world. Who could not believe in that?

The Blessed mother is our forever advocate, and praying to her is an indispensable way of enhancing our faith. She is not to be worshipped, but rather to be prayed to, our pipeline of supplication, where we hope she will not only listen to us, but also answer our petitions. Her special prayer, the *Memorare*, is a beautiful petition, one I recite every day both privately and in our pre-Mass rosary every day. Succinct in length, it is deep in spiritual meaning and, most important, a guide to having petitions heard and answered.

"Remember, O most gracious Virgin Mary, that never was it known that anyone who fled to thy protection, implored thy help, or sought thy intercession was left unaided. Inspired with this confidence, I fly to thee, O Virgin of virgins, my Mother; to thee do I come; before thee I stand, sinful and sorrowful. O Mother of the Word Incarnate, despise not my petitions, but in thy mercy hear and answer me. Amen."

Blessed Mother, we love you!

Chapter 4:
Acquiring and Growing in My Faith

"Three things are necessary to everyone: Truth of faith, which brings understanding; love of Christ, which brings compassion; and endurance of hope, which brings perseverance".

(Saint Bonaventure)

All I have written prior to this chapter might seem, at times, superfluous, but I have included the material as an exposition of all I believe and accept unequivocally, beginning with the very tenet that God exists and loves us without reservation.

As Father Aidan Kavanagh said many times in his classes at Yale, "Grace does not come down from heaven in a Glad bag." No, it comes from the Holy Spirit and becomes an intrinsic presence in our hearts and minds. Once we accept the unalienable fact that God's existence makes no sense and never can or should, then we are on our way to a lifelong journey of ever-increasing our faith.

I would be lying if I said I loved God from the moment I was told about him. No, it was a step-by-step process that had numerous days of doubts about his being who he is, or why the Church imposed such strict behavioral rules on us, or even why we could or could not do certain things that our spiritual leaders condemned as morally harmful or mortally sinful.

Too many times, I have heard that the Church's strictures regarding morality are just man-made rules. However, what the Church asks of us as Catholics through its rules are not capriciously brought to us as punishments, an effort by religious leaders to control our every action, or any other nonsense. No, they are firmly based on Jesus' teachings and are promulgated by cardinals and the pope only after long debates, changes within each one, and then a one hundred percent consensus. The presence of the Holy Spirit at those discussions guarantees that what is finally decided is good for everyone, from the pope to us as laymen and women.

I knew nothing about Church laws, rules, expectations or commandments at an early age. While that in itself is not unusual, and I was born as what is known as a "cradle Catholic," my parents never went near a church for many years, except for weddings and funerals. Well, what did I know? They did not teach me the rosary, prayers, or faith practices. So, my life for a time was totally devoid of even the concept of do's and don'ts of the Church.

My earliest knowledge of what God expects of us came instead from nuns, who were my first teachers of religious matters. Just as we have teachers in school to impart knowledge of English standards, math, history and other subjects, so too do we have priests, nuns, and Catholic scholars. They introduce us to God's will and commandments, as well as to how we are to behave morally and ethically. Without them, there could never be any cohesive structure.

As a very young child, I had yet to understand even an iota of what God or the Church meant. Let me show how naïve I was. My mother took me to a wedding Mass when I was three or four years old. I had never seen a priest prior to that day, and I was puzzled by what he was wearing. I said, as loud as could be, "Mommy, why is that man wearing a dress?" She was probably looking for the nearest trap door after that outburst, but honestly, I don't remember if there was laughter or any other reaction. Out of the mouths of babes...

Fast-forward a few years and I found myself in preparation class for making First Confession and First Holy Communion. My classmates and I attended public school, so we had no religious instruction that a parochial school offers. We then were introduced to the good Sisters, nuns who came to our church. Saint Bernadette's in New Haven, Connecticut, once a week to teach all the classes.

We all soon learned they carried not only prayer books, but very un-church-like rulers. If any of us laughed out of turn, made a snide remark or committed any other deviant action in their eyes the offending boy (mostly) or girl suffered from very sore knuckles.

I must admit I cannot remember if I ever went home with stars of pain shooting from my knuckles, but you might say that just the thought of being whacked was an especially stern warning to pay strict attention and behave.

Those nun-driven sessions were to be the foundation of our prayer life, and indeed they were exactly that. By reciting, over and over, the Our Father, Hail Mary, Act of Contrition and other basic prayers, I and the others proudly displayed our newly found knowledge by reciting those prayers to our parents when we returned home. My parents listened patiently to my recitations every time and never failed to tell me what a good job I was doing in memorizing those prayers.

A few years later, my mother and father did return to the Faith, and my mother happily told me it was because I had become such a good attendee. I was thrilled, but could not take credit for the change of heart my parents underwent. Guess who nudged them – yep, the Holy Spirit, my pal.

Back to age seven, where the good Sisters advised us that we had reached the age of reason, whatever that meant. Only some years later did I get to know the book by Thomas Paine with that same title. Of course, that was a different topic entirely.

At my pre-pre puberty age, the only reason I knew was when I got turned down by my mother or father for something I wanted. When I asked for a reason, I got the usual answer: "Because I said so." All parents go to the same school to learn those and other responses, and all kids have to accept them, perhaps grudgingly, but necessarily. Being sent to bed without supper was never a good option.

In any event, I had reached the nebulous concept called the age of reason. To this day, I have no idea why the Church proclaimed it to be at such a young age In fact, even the Church leaders are vague in the definition. Here is what one Catholic source says:

"There is no hard-and-fast rule for determining the age of reason: it is a judgment call on the part of parents, pastors and teachers — the ones who know the child the best. In general, throughout the United States, second grade is the time when children receive first Communion. Typically, the children in second grade are between the ages of 7 and 9." (simplycatholic.com/age-of-reason)

Fine, but what is reason? At ages seven through nine, my head and all others in my age group were filled with more important matters, such as when we would have pizza again, whether we could skip homework to watch our favorite children's TV program, or what gifts we would get for our birthday or Christmas. Worldly thoughts certainly did not intrude on other issues, including the age of reason.

That brings me back to the good Sisters in our church basement every week, who brought with them not only prayer books and those frightening rulers, but also stern warnings as they prepared us for First Confession and First Holy Communion.

Solemnly, they poured fire and brimstone onto us. Everything was a mortal sin, in their eyes. You lie, it is a mortal sin. You use bad words, it is a mortal sin. Disobeying parents, teachers and other adults was also a terrible sin. And – most damning of all – when you receive your First Holy Communion, if you chew the Host, it is a guaranteed journey to the bowels of the Earth for all eternity.

Let's be realistic. Mortal sin certainly exists in innumerable forms, from adultery to murder, cheating, excess in gambling, drinking, drugs and other wanton pleasures, mistreating our children or spouses, and so forth. So, Jesus' words, which take precedence over what the nuns hammered at us, do not negate what they preached, but clarify them. The Lord's messages to the people spoke of hope for eternity. Yes, he warned his listeners about the consequences of serious sin, but always left the gate of heaven open to all faithful and sinless believers.

Jesus' condemnation of the Pharisees and the Jewish leaders was a direct result of their hardened hearts. Nonetheless, he extended the hope to them that if they changed their ways, reformed and repented, wonderful rewards awaited. Alas, it is doubtful that few, if any, followed his advice. In an oblique way, the good nuns taught us much the same thing Jesus tried to teach the Pharisees and other Jewish leaders. Over time, the Sisters' well-intentioned words became more and more meaningful to me.

I found somewhat of a parallel to what the Sisters warned us about on You Tube one night. A young man, who appeared to be in his early twenties, was pontificating about the dangers of kissing a woman passionately. To underscore what he was promoting, he showed a still shot of a young man kissing the cheek of a young woman. He said that was acceptable, but anything more, such as lip-kissing, was a mortal sin. That might have been over the top, but what he was trying to say was that lip-kissing could become passionate and lead to immoral acts. After I heard what he said, I wondered if he was a nun in his last life.

Of course, I am being facetious about his last life. We get one shot at earning God's eternal grace, not many. Someone – who did believe in reincarnation – asked me if I believed in a second life on Earth. I told him, "No, I don't believe in reincarnation, and I didn't believe it in my last life, either." He didn't know what to say to that.

Actually, I do believe in reincarnation, but not in that sense. Jesus himself promised several times, as John wrote in his gospel, a rising from the dead, not to another life here, but rather in the Kingdom:

"Amen, amen, I say to you, whoever keeps my word will never see death." (8:51)

(Presaging the institution of the Eucharist) *"This is the bread that came down from heaven... whoever eats this bread will live forever."* (6:58)

(The promise of eternal life while reassuring Martha before Jesus raised her brother Lazarus from the dead) *"I am the resurrection and the life; whoever believes in me, even if he dies, will live, and everyone who lives and believes in me will never die."* (11:25-26)

So yes, there is a reincarnation, one which awakens up from the sleep of our earthly death to the never-ending joys in heaven, where sadness, illness and other of life's woes are gone forever. Those nuns from my childhood at least assured us if we obeyed God, our parents, teachers and others, and did not fall into grave sin, we would be elevated to heaven as soon as we died.

As discussed above, mortal sin was not a concern to our young minds, even though the Sisters scared the daylights out of us for many other reasons. We were all doomed forever if we committed mortal sins, never to laugh or be happy again, just burn forever in the fires of hell. (Sob!)

Yet, Jesus said if we believe in Him we will never die. We should never take those words from the Lord as a *carte blanche* to lead a sinful life. Our ascension to eternal joy is the end result of leading a good moral and ethical life, being kind to and helping others, and being role models of faith to family, friends and all whose lives we touch.

It is important to close this chapter by reminding ourselves that God forgives the gravest sin, even at the point of death, as noted in a previous chapter. Just remember Dismas, hanging on a cross next to Jesus, condemned for his heinous sins against the state. While he at first might have joined the other criminal in excoriating Jesus, he was touched by the Holy Spirit and asked for forgiveness from the Lord (Luke 23:40-43). Instead of berating Jesus, Dismas did just that instead to the other criminal, reminding him that they had been condemned justly for their evil deeds. Then, in total remorse and now believing in the Lord, he said:

"Jesus, remember me when you come into your kingdom." Jesus, always all-forgiving, responded, *"Amen, I say to you, today you will be with me in Paradise".*

The Lord did not say, "Tough. You sinned badly and were a wanton criminal all your life, and now, at the point of death, you want forgiveness? Forget about it!" I challenge you to find a more poignant or graphic example of the infinite nature of the expiating of even the worst sins. Saint Dismas (as the Church venerates him) was proof that there is no limit to God's accepting our sincere confession and plea to be brought back into his grace.

Once, I was having a conversation with a man who never attended Mass, though he had been raised Catholic. He said he would make a deathbed confession instead. I tried to tell him death might occur in bed, but suppose it came in the form of an auto accident, a sudden and fatal fall, or any other circumstance that ended his life without the chance to fulfill that notion he held. Dead silence. I have always hoped that what I said to him resonated positively.

Being always in God's grace is why Jesus instituted the Sacrament of Penance after his resurrection. (John 20:22-23). Confession, now called Reconciliation by the Church, is indeed good for the soul. All sins, mortal and venial, are forgiven when the priest imparts absolution. Just as important, it is a painless and comforting way to have God restore us to His grace and love. It is a Sacrament I receive regularly, and it is now time to discuss my experiences with it and also why I embrace it to the depths of my soul and with joy and hope.

Chapter 5:
Behind closed doors (or a closed curtain)

"Receive the Holy Spirit. Whose sins you forgive are forgiven them, and whose sins you retain are retained."
(Jesus in John 20:23, instituting the Sacrament of Divine Forgiveness)

Unexpectedly, while contemplating what to write about hope and the Sacrament of Reconciliation, I found the answer in – of all places – a cryptogram puzzle. Please let me explain.

When I am writing or doing research for a project, I relax by challenging myself with Cryptograms, which look like gibberish but are letters disguised as other letters. A puzzle book is the last place I expected to find a statement apropos to this chapter on the Sacrament of Reconciliation. Indeed, the quote that follows hits directly on one the outcomes for which we wish by confessing our sins – hope.

Chinmoy Kumar Ghose (1931-2007), a Hindu, penned the words, which are so meaningful to anyone who keep hope in his or her heart. Born and raised in India, he moved to New York City and promoted his way to inner peace. Here is one of those beautiful sentiments:

"Hope knows no fear, Hope dares to blossom even inside the abysmal abyss. Hope secretly feels and strengthens promise."

Those almost-poetic words are ones we can all understand, agree with, and cherish. Though not a Catholic, Ghose was deeply spiritual and spent his life promoting his way to peace and happiness. In a similar way, our Sacrament of Reconciliation does the same thing to our souls.

As Catholics, we all know that one of the seven Sacraments is Penance. It is one of the three Jesus himself imparted to the eleven disciples just before and just after his Resurrection. The Lord instituted the Eucharist and Holy Orders to the disciples at the Last Supper. Forgiveness through Penance came at a post-Resurrection appearance, and remains with us, a vital and most approachable Sacrament that gives us all of God's grace and lets us receive the Eucharist worthily.

Receiving that Sacrament is central to our Catholic practices. In forgiving, God is also forgetting. What sins we confess sincerely, are forgotten forever. Confession kills sin on contact, not totally unlike one of those bug-killing sprays. It is always in complete concert with the Eucharist, because, just as with love and marriage, you can't receive the one without the other.

When I was a young pup and naïve about the amount of sin in the world out there to tempt me, my first encounter with the Sacrament of Penance came to my peers and me at age seven. As said in the previous chapter, the nuns who visited our church weekly might have been stern, but they also instilled a love of God and the Sacraments in us. They prepared us well for our first entry into that dark, curtain-lined box then called the Confessional.

Perhaps the most important prayer the Sisters taught us was the Act of Contrition. The good Sisters made us repeat it until we had it memorized, often randomly calling on one of us to recite it. They reminded us of its importance more times than we would have liked, but who was going to tell them otherwise? It was necessary, they said firmly, because the priest would have us recite it after confessing our monumental sins, and no stumbles or word omissions were allowed. In effect, they reminded us, the Act of Contrition was the final step to receiving God's grace and forgiveness.

I and the others in class were still spiritually innocent, but we figured the nuns knew what was necessary. Like anything else in life, recognition and importance come gradually, as least to me. You see, I was a little slow on the uptake. Though I memorized ninety-nine percent of the Act of Contrition fairly easily, I completely misunderstood one small part at the beginning of the Act.

We were taught to say, "O my God, I am heartily sorry for having offended Thee". For reasons I still cannot explain all these decades later, I thought the opening was, "O my God, I am *partly* sorry for having offended Thee." Whoops!

Strangely, the priest either never understood what I was whispering (as we all did back in the late 1940s in the confessional), or he wrote it off to my youthful ignorance. For years afterward, even into my teens, I said "partly sorry" instead of "heartily sorry."

Then, one day the light bulb went on. It was about a 40-watt variety, but enough to show me the error of my ways. I was thumbing through a prayer book I found on a shelf in my parents' home and came across the Act of Contrition. What followed next was the religious version of sticker shock. I read the Act and my jaw dropped to the floor when I saw "Heartily"?! No question; I was consigned to eternal punishment over a single, but badly misused word. Needless to say, my next visit behind the curtain ended with my newly discovered word – the correct one. I know

God understood that my past misuse was accidental and not deliberate.

Underscoring that is something I found on the Catholic website, find2god.com/confession. Just as a washing machine cleans clothes, confession washes away our sins, as the following says (boldface by the anonymous author):

*"Confession is a difficult but necessary part of faith and spiritual growth. Confessing one's sins to God is about more than just relieving guilt. This act helps us grow closer to Him again. **Through the sacrament of confession and the washing clean of all sins, one returns to the state of sanctifying grace,** which has been given at Baptism. This state is also described in the Bible as a wedding garment. In sanctifying grace we are one with God. As in the state of grave sin, we are separated from Him. That is why it is so important to regularly confess one's sins repentantly in Holy Confession."*

So many times, I have heard something like this: "I make an Act of Contrition before Communion. That is good enough." Well, it is good, but not close to being enough. I would be less than honest if I did not say I have never done that myself. I was in a relationship with a woman about a year after my wife's death, and we ended up in the same bed a number of times. Not sex, but we played "baseball", reaching third base, if you know what I mean.

Wracked with guilt, and being a daily communicant, I justified doing those acts by making an Act of Perfect Contrition at Mass before receiving the Eucharist. Idiot! Who was I kidding?

Just what is that prayer? Is it different from the usual Act of Contrition? One Sacramental expert explained this in an article published in the Catholic News Agency on March 27, 2020, and written by Jonah McKeown. This excerpt from that article puts a stamp of absoluteness on why even an Act of Perfect Contrition does in no way replace going to Confession.

"Father Pius Pietrzyk, OP, chair of pastoral studies at St. Patrick's Seminary in Menlo Park, California, told CNA that 'perfect contrition' is sorrow for one's sins based upon love for God, which includes the firm resolution not to commit them any more.

"When contrition arises from 'a love by which God is loved above all else, contrition is called 'perfect,' the Catechism of the Catholic Church teaches. The catechism explains that perfect contrition 'remits venial sins; it also obtains forgiveness of mortal sins if it includes the firm resolution to have recourse to sacramental confession as soon as possible'. Imperfect co contrition, also known as attrition- sorrow for one's sins based upon fear of the punishment of Hell- is sufficient for a priest to absolve you in the confessional, but not enough to obtain the forgiveness of mortal sin without sacramental confession to a priest, the catechism explains.'"

The reason for that longish citation and my own admission for justifying in my pea brain that yes, I did something sinful, perhaps mortally sinful, and had to go to Confession. I did just that – several times – and sometimes relapsed when in the company of that woman. Finally, I listened to my confessor, a wonderful monsignor, who gently told that even in my later stage of life, what I was engaging in was completely unacceptable and very sinful. You can't fool or cheat God.

In a way, you could say that by admitting the above action, I made a confession to you, the reader, and you would be right. However, it was not a *Sacramental* confession. The Sacrament of Penance/Reconciliation can be conferred only be an ordained priest or bishop, not by a person's private expression of sorrow.

Yes, when we confess to the good priest, we are saying we will not repeat those sins again. An amusing – and fictional – example of promising not to repeat a serious sin involved a man who was a compulsive thief, constantly stealing lumber. Feeling very guilty, he finally went to Confession and told of his misdeed to the priest, fervently promising never to steal lumber again. After giving the man absolution, the priest, before conferring the man's penance, asked, "Do you know how to make a novena?" The man replied eagerly, "No, Father, but if you give me the plans, I can steal the lumber."

Not exactly the smartest way to rid one of his sins.

Over my life, I have been blessed by a number of holy, understanding, and gentle confessors. In every confession I have ever made, I have always promised not to commit those sins I just revealed to the priests ever again. Here is the problem: I am human, just everyone else. I am an imperfect being, often so tempted to do the wrong thing, though most often succeeding in not repeating a serious sin. At times, I fell from grace, but again restored myself to God by confessing to the priest at the earliest I could.

As we all know only too well, the devil is always there, plying us with prurient pleasure thoughts, and telling us it is okay to sin. Sometimes, we do, recidivating and breaking our promise to the priest. Hopeless situation? Not at all. That is why God's forgiveness is always there for us. A lapse, even back to serious sin, is always forgivable, but I must make whatever effort is necessary to eliminate that sin forever from my life. It is not easy, but if I keep my eyes on the ultimate reward, I can and will do it.

When I moved from Connecticut to Naples, Florida, in the year 2021, I searched for a church to attend the day after I settled in to my new condo. The Holy Spirit, my ever-present companion, showed me one not far from my residence. Saint Peter the Apostle became my new parish immediately. Its priests, I discovered were friendly, theologically conservative and orthodox in every respect, and always eager to listen to any need, especially the forgiving of sins.

I mention that because without exception, all five priests assigned to my church are points of brilliant light in the Room of Reconciliation. Their advice after I confess to them is always gentle, positive, and yet a bit cautionary at the same time. Thank you, Spirit, for guiding me to this wonderful parish, where I quickly embrace every aspect of it, even to teaching courses on the parables of Jesus and attending many of the other courses others present. Love it!

No matter how old you are, the expression, "Confession is good for the soul", applies and is right on the money. Best of all, it means receiving God's forgiveness and leaving the room where the Sacrament is conferred feeling ten feet tall and like a new person.

Back in the 1940s and until after Vatican II in the 1960s, confession could be an almost terrifying experience. Some priests questioned our sin admissions with raised voices that all standing outside the dark box (no Room of Reconciliation back then) could hear. The curtain we brushed aside going in and out of the confessional did nothing to diminish the sound of the stern lecture we might be receiving.

Making my First Confession was not too difficult, because the pastor understood we were just rank beginners at this practice and went easy on us. That changed as we grew a bit older.

I can still vividly remember the worst experience I ever had in that dark box, in my late teenage years. Little did I know that the priest hearing confessions in my church one Saturday was fairly deaf. I confessed something and he bellowed, "You're not going to quit doing that?" I emphasized in a softer voice, but not much quieter than his, "I am not going to *continue* doing that." After receiving absolution, I left the dark box, head down, hoping no one knew who I was.

Many of us in those days, often went "priest shopping," confessing to a priest who was known for light penances and a fairly quick in and out of the confessional. At my own parish back in the 1950s, the pastor was stern and pounded on the pulpit when giving a sermon. He practiced an almost a spiritual dictatorship. Needless to say, we did not enjoy having him hear about our transgressions. Outside the confessional, and on a personal level, he was kind and understanding. Well, nobody's perfect!

Confessing today is dramatically different from those stern-priest times. The modern form of confessing is in a well-lighted and welcoming setting. We have the choice of kneeling and facing a curtain hiding the priest, or sitting face-to-face with him. The old dark, curtain-clad box from earlier decades, with its darkness and an almost built-in intimidating factor, is still used in many churches, mostly at Christmastime or Easter, when more people seek forgiveness.

Now, with the Room of Reconciliation, we no longer have to whisper our transgressions or mumble and hope the priest will not question what we are saying. No, we now speak in a normal voice, and are far less than anxious to confess even the most serious sins.

While confession might not be construed as fun, it is so comforting to have a conversation with the priest, perhaps even engage in a little small talk, and then, being more relaxed, pour out our souls to him. Getting one's halo polished has become not only easier, but also such an accommodating way to bring God's love back to us.

I often wonder today how many people still recall a priest or two who intimidated or chastised them in a way they found so intimidating that they never went to confession again. Perhaps they thought the Act of Contrition was sufficient for forgiveness. They have little or no idea as to how both penitent and priest now approach this beautiful Sacrament. It is the most beautiful way of receiving God's forgiveness.

What I feel in my own heart is gratitude, not only for having this wonderful gift from Jesus himself, but also because how welcoming and nonthreatening the Church has made the process. Yes, there is always a bit of trepidation and perhaps embarrassment over confessing a particularly serious sin, and believe me, I know that feeling firsthand.

On the other hand, as someone once told me, the priest has heard it all before and is not judgmental. He is there as the representative of Jesus Christ, who, through the priest, forgives our sins, mortal and venial The confessor then assigns a penance, usually a number of Our Fathers and Hail Marys, or something similar, which we are obligated to say before receiving Communion again.

Confession is neither a chore nor a dreaded event we have to endure as Catholics. Rather, it is, besides the Eucharist, the greatest expression of love and sorrow we can express to God, through the aegis of the priest. I try to visit the Room of Reconciliation monthly, preceded by a lengthy examination of conscience, as well as asking the Holy Spirit to enlighten my memory so I don't forget to confess everything. The end result, after the priest absolves my sins, is the greatest feeling of peace I could possibly have. Being in God's grace is a wonderful achievement.

Chapter 6:
Mass and the Eucharist – a "Marriage" of One Rite, One Beloved Sacrament

"Oh, what awesome mysteries take place during Mass! One day we will know what God is doing for us in each Mass, and what sort of gift He is preparing in it for us. Only His divine love could permit that such a gift be provided for us. O Jesus, my Jesus, with what great pain is my soul pierced when I see this fountain of life gushing forth with such sweetness and power for each soul, while at the same time I see souls withering away and drying up through their own fault. O Jesus, grant that the power of mercy embraces these souls."

—*St. Maria Faustina Kowalska*

During the 1950s and even decades earlier, love songs predominated on the radio and in band music at dances, weddings and other gala occasions. One in particular applies to this discussion – "Love and Marriage." All I ask is that you not have me sing the lyrics. My voice will never be acceptable for the choir of angels.

The opening lines of that long-ago song were: "Love and marriage, love and marriage, go together like a horse and carriage. This I tell ya [sic], brother – you can't have one without the other."

No real spiritual message there, but in a very different way the Mass and Eucharist also go together, and you can't have one without the other. The Lord himself celebrated the first-ever Mass at the Last Supper. It was during this rite that he consecrated bread and wine, which became his Body and Blood, Soul and Divinity. No greater miracle than the Consecration can ever exist.

I have often wondered why so many people view the beautiful sacrifice we call the Mass as merely a weekend obligation, little more. I would bet my pension (which won't put you in even a cheap used car, by the way) that you cannot tell me you have never heard the following in some form or other: "Let's go to the 8 o'clock Mass and get it over with." But I definitely would lose that meager income if you tell me you *have* heard, "Let's go out to have a good time and get it over with." My pension is safe.

I am not throwing any stones, because like all other human beings I have had questions about the Mass, such as why the readings, Gloria, Creed, and even the homily are necessary. Many times when I was much younger, I wondered why the pope would not declare that the Mass was to be just the presentation of the gifts of bread, water and wine, and the blessings and Consecration, followed by reception of Communion and the prayer of dismissal. Great concept, I thought. In just fifteen minutes, the whole ceremony would be over and we could spend our time elsewhere, having fun or doing what we consider more productive activities.

Fortunately, I came to realize in not too long a time, that there were very good reasons for including all the parts comprising the Mass. Every one has an irreplaceable function for being in the blessed sacrifice. Yes, the Mass is a sacrifice, a direct reminder of the Last Supper and the Passion of Jesus that followed it. To truncate this beautiful sacrificial rite would be akin to almost negating its intent and meaning. No part of it is superfluous; every component, every word, is vital.

All Masses begin with the Sign of the Cross. In which we acknowledge the Holy Trinity. We then admit to being sinners and recite or sing the Gloria, a recitation or hymn of praise telling the Father, Son, and Holy Spirit that we believe in them without doubt.

Three readings follow, almost always based on the theme of that particular weekend Mass. During most of the year, the first reading is from a book of the Old Testament, and the second one is from a book in the New Testament. We then stand to honor God as the celebrant or deacon reads the gospel.

Why those readings? Why not just go to the gospel and eliminate the other two, as well as the Responsorial Psalm? Good question, and there is a good answer. The first reading at Masses during what is called Ordinary Time reveals actions, faith matters, prophets' predictions and other revelatory information, mostly from the Old Testament. The second reading focuses on excerpts from Saint Paul's epistles, the Book of Acts, or other letters and even Revelation. They are meant to enhance both our knowledge of spiritual matters, and enlighten us, deepening our faith.

Ditto when we hear the gospel reading and then the celebrant's or deacon's homily. What they reveal are not just ordinary words, but those of eternal life. That is why all the readings are vital to the fabric of the Mass. They prepare us to be more sacramentally aware and more eager to be a better participant in the Mass.

It took me many years to fully appreciate that critical fabric of the Mass. But when I let my eyes open to the messages those two readings were conveying, my perspective changed to an enhanced grasp and love of them.

The gospel, of course, conveys even deeper meanings. Whether the weekly gospel is a parable or an event in the life of our Savior, there are underlying and not-so-overt messages we can see, especially by studying them in our Bible at home. That is what my graduate advisor, Father Aidan Kavanagh, taught, as did other professors at the divinity school. I want to share an example of the wisdom of what one faculty member taught us regarding the parable of the wedding feast in Matthew 22:1-14.

A king was hosting a wedding feast for his son and the son's bride and had invited a large number of people to attend and celebrate with them. All the wedding guests said they would not come, and sone killed the servants he sent to ask them to attend. The enraged king killed the killers and burned down their city. He then told his servants to scour the area and being both the good and bad to the feast. Those first-invited who refused to attend were banished forever.

Once the servants had assembled those culled from highways, byways, and other places, the king saw one man not dressed in a wedding garment. When the king asked him why he was not appropriately dressed, the man had no answer. The king ordered him bound and thrown out into the dark. Jesus cautioned the chief priests, to whom he addressed the parable, saying, *"For many are called, but few are chosen."*

A cursory reading of the parable at Mass or privately might not trigger a desire to look underneath the event itself and see what unspoken messages are contained in this parable. They are there, lying beneath the surface, as the professor pointed out. He then told us the king was God, who invites every human being to attend the eternal feast – heaven. The people refusing the invitation were the Jews and others who ignored the messages the Lord preached. The king's servants represented the apostles, who were all later martyred for the Faith, The good and bad people who did accept the invitation represented all who heard and believed in Jesus' words.

What about the man not wearing a wedding garment? He tried to attend the banquet without bothering to wear appropriate clothes. His presence was abhorrent to the king, because he was not in His Majesty's grace. When Jesus told this parable to the Pharisees and chief priests, he meant it as a strong warning to them. Because of their greed, craving of power and other failings, they would be excluded from heaven. The lack of a wedding garment was not relating to clothing at all; it was symbolic of a mantle of sin.

You might wonder why the man in the parable, apparently summoned at the last minute to attend the wedding feast, was so harshly treated, just because he was not dressed appropriately. In ancient Israel the wealthy often had wedding garments reserved for guests for just such an event. So, the offender undoubtedly was given a chance to wear one to the wedding. Either he refused the garment or just wanted to enjoy a free meal.

Without seeking the subtle meanings lying beneath the words, a reader is likely to say, "That king was cruel. After all, his servants brought in people at the last minute." No, not true. A host, under those circumstances, would have delayed the feast for a time to give the newly chosen attendees a chance to freshen up, change, or accept the largess of the proffered wedding garment upon arrival at the palace.

The uncaring guest represented the Jewish leaders who were like the underdressed attendee. Their sins and lust for power and control led to their condemnation. Little wonder they were so incensed by what Jesus told them that they went off together and plotted as to how they could Kill him (Matthew 23:1). Message received and rejected. The uneducated itinerant preacher had to go.

I reflect daily on the parables of Jesus and search for underlying messages. Every one of those precious sayings of the Lord has meanings the reader can uncover through careful thought and by using an annotated Bible for even more understanding. Doing so necessarily leads to a more enlightened grasp of the words of Jesus and what he was telling all of us.

Further, I also love reading many of the Old Testament books. I lean toward the marvelous words in Sirach, the wonderful messages in Isaiah, the courage of Judith in the eponymous book about her, Daniel's adventures and great moral judgments, the reluctance (and somewhat amusing) arguments Jonah used with God when he became an unwilling prophet, and many others. The Bible stands alone as the greatest book ever written. I love every word and every story and the new meanings in the messages that I discover every time.

As we leave the discussion on the Mass readings, the Mass of the Catechumens comes to an end. (Explanation of this follows below.) We segue into the Consecration Rite, the most solemn part of the Mass, also once called the Mass of the Faithful. Those terms are still in use, but not in the same way as they were for many centuries.

In the earliest years of Christianity, the Mass of the Catechumens comprised the Gloria, prayers, and readings. All who attended the service, Christian or not, could be present. Those folks not yet baptized but eager to be Christians had to leave after the sermon. Only baptized people could participate in the second part or the rite, the Mass of the Faithful.

Today, all are welcome, no matter whether they are not members of our Church or are even nonbelievers. We embrace one and all. Our hope for nonbelievers or non-Christians who have stopped their faith practices is that the Holy Spirit envelops them with his love and grace, and they become Catechumens in preparation for baptism. They cannot receive the Eucharist, but are free to worship and receive a blessing from the celebrant at Communion time.

Following the Nicene Creed (usually that one, rather than the Apostles' Creed), the act of Consecration nears. The celebrant asks God to bless the bread, water and wine and then washes his hands. The washing is a supplication to be cleansed from sin. It also is the prelude to the Consecration, which follows the Preface after the celebrant dries his hands.

I will not reinvent the wheel by explaining the miracle that occurs when the celebrant consecrates the Host. Suffice it to say that you will note the silence in the church seems to deepen further when the celebrant says slowly and reverently, "This is my body," and then, "This is my blood," the exact words Jesus himself imparted at the first Mass and who comes into the church in full divinity after those beautiful words are uttered.

It is necessary to avoid all superlatives regarding the core of the Mass, the Consecration. How can I describe the incredible act

Jesus Christ performs when the celebrant calls him down from heaven without going overboard with praises? His Real Presence is, of course, the culmination of our faith gift, which we possess even before we enter the church. If we take this gift lightly, we are casting aside the beauty and intrinsic miracle the Lord performs.

Little matter if Mass is celebrated in the biggest cathedral or in a small room with a makeshift altar, Jesus' presence is just as real. Remember, the Last Supper was offered in the Upper Room of a private house, perhaps a deliberate act by the Lord to demonstrate the need for humility and also to remind us that his presence is everywhere.

Once again, I can state without equivocation that the Eucharist is yet another part of the reason that God's existence makes no sense. Why would Jesus, reviled, tortured and crucified, not just turn his back on the entire humanity? That would have made more sense. However, it would also negate the fact that God's love and forgiveness are unending, and that is why the Savior gave us an eternal gift for us to cherish.

Earlier, I noted that a large majority of Catholics do not believe in the Real Presence. That is beyond sad; it is tragic. Though I also went through periods of doubt about some of the Church's laws and directives, I never, ever doubted that Jesus was there in his full post-redemption glory.

Is there a secret to being more in concert with the Eucharist? Absolutely, though it is not really a secret. Simply begin with a very brief prayer to the Lord: "Jesus, I believe, Help my unbelief." Then, instead of reciting by rote the prayers in which we all participate, study their meanings privately, before attending Mass.

What underlying messages are contained in the Gloria, Nicene Creed, Lord's Prayer, and other supplications we recite? We are not robots, and the prayers are not robotics. They are filled with spiritual revelations that, when our eyes are opened more clearly to them, make our faith a living part of us, not just words to say weekly at Mass or daily at home.

One more thing and here comes another of my (infamous or famous) asides. Regarding prayer study, and leading to a more enhanced appreciation of the prayers so familiar to us, I recommend any book that you can purchase online that guides you through Catholic prayers and what they contain to make us stronger Christians. Amazon has many; Catholic religious orders also sell them.

Yes, the Mass is more than a rite and infinitely more than just a weekly obligation; it is the center of our spirituality. As the celebrant leads up to the Rite of Concentration, immerse yourself in its meaning and be in awe that Jesus himself is about to appear under the species of bread and wine. Then, as we approach the altar to receive him, give thanks for his forgiveness through confession, for keeping us from temptation, and for embracing us with a wonderful and irreplaceable gift that exists nowhere else.

Each time I attend Mass, my heart is filled with the joy of knowing my Divine Savior is about to come down from heaven and be with all who are there to worship him. Conversely, I am also deeply humbled as I reflect on my unworthiness for having been granted the grace to be in the presence of the greatest human act of bringing Jesus to us at the Consecration. This most wonderful gift from God himself has no equal whatever. Frankly,

I am awed by what a great miracle the celebrant performs each and every time.

That is why our beautiful Mass is more than an obligation or something to "get it over with." It is only true path to eternal life to be with the Holy Trinity, our Blessed Mother, and all the angels and saints. I just hope and pray I am deemed worthy to be among them.

Chapter 7:
Why Jesus is the Center of My Life

"I am the resurrection and the life; whoever believes in me, even if he dies, will live, and everyone who lives and believes in me will never die."

(John 11:25-26)

In the preceding chapter, I concluded with my deep feelings about the Mass and the miracle Jesus performs through the celebrant. Now, I want to explain a little further how Jesus became the center of my life.

Though I have always been a member of the Catholic Faith and became a daily communicant more than 40 years ago, it was not always the case. There were weeks I did not attend Mass. Admittedly, they were rare occurrences, and I confessed the sin to my priest. But there were also long stretches in my younger days – I would say in my late teens and twenties – that I never received the Eucharist because I was engaged in relishing immoral behavior, mostly by being aroused through viewing magazines featuring nude women. As I said earlier in this work, I am far from perfect. Sometimes, I wonder why God is so forgiving, but I am grateful for his grace.

Oh, there other actions that warranted confession, which I delayed for weeks and months at a time. I was too busy being one in concert with the worldly pleasures. No drugs ever entered my life, but at times I drank excessively, especially at parties. How I ever drove home from some of them still makes me shudder. I might have run over somebody, crashed into a light pole, or even been arrested for driving under the influence, but God watched over me, despite my wayward activities.

Where there is life, there is hope. God never gave up on me, and in 1969, after marrying Dorothy (or "Dottie", as she liked to be called), I became more involved in the Faith. There were still those parties and other temptations, but marriage has a unique way of leading an errant soul back into a stronger moral and ethical life.

I am ashamed to admit this, but during my early years of marriage my eye sometimes strayed and I fantasied that it would be so nice to get cozy with whatever woman I was gazing at. It never happened, even though my marriage was up and down at times, and occasionally seriously down (Aren't they all!).

I want to add for the reader's benefit that my wife was a regular churchgoer, though never a daily attendee. Neither was I for about the first few years of our married life. Then, things began to come together more deeply for me in terms of my spirituality. Not coincidentally, my eyes stopped wandering to other women.

We were husband and wife for about four years, when I decided it would be good to commemorate Lent by going to Mass more often, as I did in college. Those weekday Masses during the penitential season were just a prelude to what I embraced some years later. But again the Holy Spirit is the best guide of all. He did not rush me into anything; I had to discover the efficacy of daily Mass in good time. And I did.

There was never a time that I doubted the Real Presence of Jesus in the Blessed Sacrament, and while I cannot recapture the years when I did not become closer to Him through the Sacrament, it now is the only fulfilling way for me and others to start every morning, as it has now been for decades.

I am not bragging; there are countless numbers of daily communicants in every Catholic church, including mine – Saint Peter the Apostle Church in Naples. Discovering how daily Mass enhanced my faith, however, was not so much a life-changer as it was a life-uplifter. Jesus Christ is forever the center of my life. I am humbled by his incomparable gift of the Eucharist and, quite frankly, awed by it. I always pray just before Mass that I am receiving him worthily.

So, how do I explain my journey from a casual, innocent person believing almost vaguely in God to where I am today? Please understand I am scarcely a saint. As I said earlier, my halo – if it exists at all – will never be blinding to others.

Perhaps the best way I can explain my ever-expanding faith is through Jesus' parable of the fig tree (Luke 13:6-9). In that lesson, we find a landowner who tells his gardener to cut down the tree, which has been barren for three years. The gardener (Jesus) remonstrates with the landowner (God the Father) and asks the landowner to let him fertilize the tree. If it then produces no fruit, the landowner can then order it cut down.

The barren fig tree and I had a lot in common. Earlier, I noted I did not take my Catholic Faith totally seriously. Rather, I partied, sinned, and was hardly pleasing to God. The fig tree is symbolic of the barren soul that is riddled with sin. Giving it another chance is how confessing to a priest restores us to God's grace and helps us bear much spiritual fruit. In life, God gives us many chances to repent and be in his grace. We will only be cut down (denied heaven) if we remain barren and not remorseful. Where there is life, there is hope. Thank you, Lord.

Such endless forgiveness and unending love are always there for us. No matter how bereft we become in terms of unbelief or fail to practice our beliefs, forgiveness is there without end if and when we seek it.

That, dear reader, is yet another reason God's existence makes no sense. How many times have you heard or read about spouses, friends and others being slighted or betrayed and remaining unforgiving? Even though that is wrong, it is an unfortunate part of our human nature.

God doesn't run the ship quite that way. He is always watching, always letting us do what we please, always cherishing a sinner's return to a spiritual life. My good pal, the Holy Spirit, was the impetus and guide for me to become a more fervent practitioner. I am forever grateful.

We always think in terms of our own life experiences, good and bad. Everything is finite, from a job, a ballgame, and especially life itself. I am convinced that is one of the reasons so many have difficulty accepting the infinite and forgiving nature of our heavenly Father. That is scarcely something new; just look at the reactions of the Jewish leaders to the teaching and preaching of Jesus. The parallels between rejecting God then and now are not at all dissimilar.

It is so easy to think and feel that our good times, our neglecting God, and hurrying along our own way are never to end. Paradoxically, we also know our time in this life is limited. So, why not surrender our souls completely to God? Again, human nature tends to ignore the end times we all someday face and tells us to focus on getting rich, living a good life with all the "perks" that go with it, and deluding ourselves by thinking. This will last forever!" Not quite.

Recall the parable of the rich man with his bountiful harvest (Luke 12:16-21). In his fantasy he imagined he would be more than comfortable for many years, with his bigger barns and plenty of wheat and other crops to eat. The lap of luxury awaited him. Unfortunately for him, his "future" ended hours later.

Similarly, the Scribes and Pharisees craved never-ending power and control. A huge part of the reason those leaders rejected the Lord had to do with the message Jesus delivered over and over. His was a mission of peace, humility, and love. That was the polar opposite of what the Jewish leaders followed in their lives. Pharisees, scribes and chief priests were mostly wealthy and power-hungry.

Even though the Roman Empire occupied Israel, politically the Jewish leaders accommodated them, probably fearing that if they engaged in anti-Roman behavior, their end would not be pretty. They thought they had it made and their glory days would never end.

Then, along came this formally uneducated preacher, who proceeded to turn their world of greed and power upside down. Everything he did, in the minds of the Pharisees, Scribes, and Sadducees was unlawful. Why, he cured illness and disabilities on the Sabbath. How dare he! That was proscribed in Mosaic law. He further infuriated them by putting them down in arguments with a few well-chosen words. He preached love and forgiveness and humility. And worst of all, he claimed to be the Son of God. Horror to end all horrors!

This is yet another example of God making no sense. Why would an infinitely loving God send his Son to earth, to be born of humble circumstances, be rejected by so many despite all the miracles and words of love he imparted, and eventually be crucified between two thieves? Let's be honest – that does require a giant leap of faith.

Little wonder many today scoff at Jesus being the Word made flesh or, as some have opined, if he existed at all. When we accept this Savior and embrace him in life, we have indeed made that leap of faith. It further means that when we fully accept the premise that God's existence makes no sense, then we have forever realized that his non-logical existence is the underscoring reason as to why we believe.

A stronger example of belief versus non-belief is found at the crucifixion itself. As he hung on that cross of infamy, he was mocked by the Jewish leaders and other passersby sneered and mocked him, saying, *"He saved others; he cannot save himself. Let the Messiah, the King of Israel, come down now from the cross that we may see and believe."* (Mark 15:31-32)

Let us put ourselves at that gruesome scene. Would we not form that same question in our minds? If he only came off the cross, unscathed and said, "Now will you believe in me?" ironically, the answer would be "No," and we have proof of that in Luke (19:31) where Jesus compared the fates of an uncaring rich man to the earthly suffering of a beggar named Lazarus. Though it was a parable, not a real-life event the Lord described, it was at the same time a dire warning to the Pharisees to whom he addressed the parable.

The rich man, consigned forever to hell and tormented by the everlasting fire, begged Abraham to send Lazarus to his five brothers. Seeing Lazarus, the rich man said, they will repent of their own sins, seeing a dead man suddenly among them. But Abraham, not at all moved by this empty plea, told the rich man, *"If they will not listen to Moses and the prophets, neither will they be persuaded if someone should rise from the dead".*

Using that parable as a fictional example of nonbelieving, Jesus subtly predicted what would occur later, at the end of his earthly ministry on the cross. Sure enough, those mocking him at the cross blithely told the Lord they would become believers if he saved himself. Again, we might have nodded our heads in total agreement if we also were standing there. If so, we would have been dead wrong.

Seeing is not always believing. The Jewish leaders would not have believed even if Jesus had exited the cross. Likely, they might have said, "His friends pretended to have him nailed, but did not use real nails. On cue, he would have come back to the ground and we were supposed to believe in him."

Further proof of unbelief was when Jesus performed his most stupendous miracle, raising Lazarus from the dead. This occurred in front of a large crowd, and some began to believe in him. Not so the Pharisees and chief priests, especially Caiphas, who said Jesus had to be put to death to save the nation from their losing control over the people. The Sanhedrin determined it was time to kill the Lord. (John 11:45-53)

Would they have embraced Jesus had they been at the tomb of Lazarus? Not at all. They were so worried about losing their power that they figured it was more expedient to rid their nation of this "troublemaker" and keep control over the Jews for the rest of their lives.

God makes no sense, and those two accounts put an indelible stamp on it. There is absolutely not an iota of logic in what a loving God did with his Son. So, are we to believe that there is a God at all, and that he is cruel to a co-equal Person, sending him to Earth just to be rejected, tortured, and then executed? Yes, we are, because God's ways are not ours. It might be difficult to accept the Creator and his method of showing us how to attain salvation, and our journey might well be fraught with suffering, pain, tragedies and other issues.

Unpleasant, at best? Unaccepted, at worst? Of course. We are human and God fully understands that our suffering might not be endured without complaining or railing against him. But just as in our own existence, anything worth attaining is worth all that befalls us. It is not easy to understand why bad things happen, but remember that, as Saint Paul said, an eternal reward awaits those who stay the course.

My own life has not been a bed of roses, for sure. It included job losses, major illnesses that I and other family members had, tragedies in and out of the household, and disappointments galore. At times, I almost railed at God because of a rapid succession of upheavals in our lives as a family. Had I not made Christ my anchor, that might well have happened. Those bitterly nasty times faded into memories, and though my wife's passing and financial difficulties arose almost without letup during her seven-year devolving mentally because of Alzheimer's disease, I thanked God I somehow was able to deal with them.

Faith is a beautiful and life-saving thing. I never stopped believing, and never will.

Recall the phrase at the beginning of this work: *"To those who believe, no explanation is necessary. To those who do not believe, no explanation is possible."* And those famous words from our Lord to Doubting Thomas:

"Blessed are they who have not seen, yet have believed." (John 20:29) Amen.

Chapter 8:
Faith is Like a Garden – We Never Stop Growing In It

"A garden is an archetypal image of the soul, of innocence, of happiness; it is a place for growth of the inner self."

(Anonymous)

Back in my high school days, one beloved teacher imparted an invaluable lesson to his students. It was simple, but effective, and to this day I still practice it. He said, *"You never stop growing in knowledge. Each day, try to learn new facts and new words. Your mind will be a garden of knowledge, which will never stop growing."*

Although I did not take his advice immediately, in college I quickly came to realize that my classmates were constantly doing research beyond classroom requirements, and often when I engaged one or more of them in a discussion, I felt like the proverbial fifth wheel; I was far behind their intellectual knowledge and accomplishments, a stark reminder that I was not engaging to the same extent in the same serious academic pursuits.

You see, in high school I chose to be a class clown and not take my courses too seriously. (My slightly older cousin at the same high school DID take his studies and was accepted to Yale. At least, I did not do anything that would send me to jail!) Making others laugh and goofing off seemed more important to "fitting in" with my peers, instead of putting my nose into books and concentrating on my studies. I won't lie; it was one of the dumbest moves I ever made.

Unfortunately for me, that academic laziness carried over to my first two years in college. More important, in my first two years of studies at the University of Bridgeport I found other activities, from football games to off-campus parties, much more enticing. The worst part was, I saw nothing wrong with any of it. After all, isn't college the best time to have fun and let everything else slide?

Reality then came to me. I would love to say I had a divine slap in the head or a k.i.t.a. (kick in the...) from above, or an epiphany that jarred me both in education and faith practice, but that was not what happened. My reversal came through a young man named John Albert, who was a classmate at UB. John was up for a good time, but also was quite serious about his studies. Because we had so much in common, including our Catholic Faith, we became friends quickly, and he and I began having extensive discussions about everything from politics to news events and classroom assignments.

When Lent came around in our freshman year, John suggested attending Mass at a local church in Bridgeport. I agreed, and every day we were in the pew participating in the then-Latin Mass. We continued that practice for two more Lenten seasons. During the third, John told me he was entering the seminary to study for the priesthood. That aroused my interest, and I also decided the priesthood was for me, as well. (More in the next chapter.)

It would be great to say that attending daily Mass with John made me a daily communicant forever, but that was not to be until years later. Once Lent was over, Sunday Mass was it for me until

I hit my forties. For many years prior to that I was satisfied with that arrangement. In fact, attending daily Mass did not even enter into my head. After all, there were parties to attend, dates to be had, and other calls from the world to be answered and embraced. At that juncture in my life I did not have God at the center of my life.

To this day, I am convinced that if I had never met John or become friends with him, God might not ever have taken the hold on my life he eventually did. Believing in God and the Sacraments of the Church was never an issue to me; I always loved them once I understood their incredible significance.

Putting my spiritual life into a more inclusive daily practice was the main obstacle. As I said above in this chapter, the call of the good life was difficult to ignore. So, that became my main focus before John Albert and I crossed paths. He was the one main person for causing a life-changing shift in spiritual attitude and, in the long run, my life.

Over the years after we went in separate career directions, John and I saw each other infrequently. Then, in the early 1980s, we stopped seeing each other altogether. No issues; those things happen sometimes, even with the closest of friends. So many times I tried to locate him without success. Then, I did a name search on the internet and was shocked to discover my great friend had been called home to God in the year 2014. Though it was a sad discovery, I will be grateful forever for his loyal friendship and his spiritual influence. I will always remember how John indirectly showed me a garden of faith that has never stopped growing.

Blessed Anne Catherine Emmerich (1774-1824), an Augustinian nun, put the word "garden" into a vivid exposition. In her book, "The Life and Revelations of Anne Catherine Emmerich", I offer the following excerpt that brings more clarity to that word in its spiritual sense.

"Our Lord, by descending into hell, planted (if I may thus express myself), in the spiritual garden of the Church, a mysterious tree, the fruits of which—namely, His merits—are destined for the constant relief of the Poor Souls in Purgatory.

"The Church Militant must cultivate the tree, and gather its fruits, in order to present them to that suffering portion of the Church which can do nothing for itself. Thus it is with all the merits of Christ; we must labor with Him if we wish to obtain our share of them; we must gain our bread by the sweat of our brow.

"Everything which Our Lord has done for us in time must produce fruit for eternity; but we must gather these fruits in time, without which we cannot possess them in eternity. The Church is the most prudent and thoughtful of mothers; the ecclesiastical year is an immense and magnificent garden, in which all those fruits for eternity are gathered together, that we may make use of them in time.

"Each year contains sufficient to supply the wants of all; but woe be to that careless or dishonest gardener who allows any of the fruit committed to his care to perish; if he fails to turn to a proper account those grace which would restore health to the sick, strength to the weak, or furnish food to the hungry! When the Day of Judgment arrives, the Master of the garden will demand a strict account, not only of every tree, but also of all the fruit produced in the garden."

It sometimes takes a saint to show us the path to happiness and beyond. Those highly symbolic words by Anne Catherine Emmerich are more than fanciful; they put our lives as "gardeners" into a beautiful perspective.

Chapter 9:
A Priesthood Never Achieved

"The Lord has sworn and not waver: Like
Melchizedek, you are a priest forever."

(Psalm 110:4)

John Albert and I were both in our junior year at UB when the call came to us from the Holy Spirit to explore a vocation to the priesthood. John mentioned it to me one day after a class, and it lit a fire within me, as well. John wanted to join the seminary for the Archdiocese of New York in Yonkers. For him, the decision was easy. His goal was to be a parish priest. For reasons I never have been able to explain, I did not want to be a parish priest, so I bought a book on the various orders in the United States.

Looking back, I probably spent as much time poring over the contents of that book as I did studying for exams at school. Hmmm… That might partially explain my less-than-stellar grades for my junior year. The Fathers of the Catholic Press caught my attention. As a budding writer, that sounded like the order I wanted to join.

Several others also were most attractive, but in the end it was the Paulist Fathers congregation that had the most of what I wanted. They had a publishing arm and were all over the United States and in Rome. Their mission was shepherding Americans, and they had locations in many states. I had made up my mind. That order was my future life – or so I thought.

My parents, especially my mother, were beyond thrilled that their older son was to be one of God's shepherds. At that time (1959), they had a small Italian pastry shop in Meriden, Connecticut, a city in the central part of the state and a branch of my uncle's main shop near New Haven. Every customer, without exception, had to listen to my mother say, "That is my son. He's going into the seminary in September." After a few weeks of that, I took to retreating to the back room whenever a customer entered the store, where I could not hear this well-intentioned but tedious (to me) mantra.

My level of enthusiasm could not have been higher. September, when I was to enter the Paulist Father's minor seminary, never seemed to arrive. Prior to leaving for Baltimore, Maryland, where the minor seminary was located, I bought the required cassock, work boots for the weekly work period, and a new tennis racket. Yes, the seminary had two tennis courts and a good-size ballfield. Seminarians don't spend all day on their knees.

The day before I was to have my parents drive me to St. Peter's Seminary in Baltimore, Maryland, my mother bought a very nice whipped cream cake (yummy!) and invited relatives and friends over for the occasion. It was quite a shock when I hugged her to thank her for the beautiful cake, and she said tearfully, "Don't go!"

Despite my mother's tearful plea, my parents drove me to the minor seminary to begin my priestly formation. It took a while to find the facility, which was located in a remote part of the city. In fact, we stopped at a gas station for directions, and I told one of the attendants I was looking for Saint Peter's Seminary. Guess he wasn't Catholic, because he said, "Oh, there's a big cemetery about a mile down the road from here." Fortunately, his coworker knew what I wanted, and he was familiar with the location. I wasn't quite ready to inhabit any cemetery.

When we finally arrived at Saint Peter's, some fellow seminarians, who had joined the Paulists a year earlier, greeted me with open arms. Any anxiety I had felt dissipated immediately. I felt accepted and welcomed.

Once we newcomers were settled and getting acclimated to St. Peter's, the rector, a no-nonsense but caring priest named Edward Gleason assembled all second-year students to an opening session. We second-year students were called "Rhets," because the focus was on rhetoric in English and religion classes. First-year students were called "Poets". Their classes focused on some poetry, though the designation was not as inclusive as with the rhetoric students.

If you are wondering why I was placed in a second-year set of classes despite it being just my first year, placements were based on the number of college years an entering seminarian had completed. One was all that was required; I had finished three.

Back to that initial get-together. Father Gleason gave us some sage advice and also cautioned us when he said, mostly to the new students, that all seminarians feel a "first fervor", in which they are gung-ho for their studies and their vocation. After a time, that fervor wanes to an extent, and doubts about having a vocation might set in. I thought it couldn't happen to me; I had found a path in life I would trod forever. Was I ever wrong! "Never say never" surely had its roots in what began to happen toward the end of my Rhett year.

I began to have my head turned slightly by thoughts of girls I had left back in Connecticut. A month later, when I returned home for summer break, worldly things I had set aside to become a priest began invading my thoughts. Making things even messier was meeting a girl at a wedding that summer. She was gorgeous and liked me. I confess I felt the same way about her. Then, I made the mistake of telling my mother, who exploded, yelling, "No! You're going to be a priest!" Her intensity left no room for debate, so I quickly dropped the subject.

Well, that did not go well. As the day neared for my entering the novitiate in rural New Jersey that fall, I was totally conflicted. Part of me wanted to go on with my priestly studies, but another part brought me thoughts of being with someone and falling in love. The novitiate ultimately won out, though it was more to please my mother than to continue pursuing a priestly vocation.

I probably should have admitted to my parents that I just not feel the seminary was for me, but – perhaps foolishly – I decided to give it my best. I convinced myself that maybe I would be so caught up in studies and the sacramental life that all would be well. It did not go that way at all.

For the next ten months, I tried to be the best novice possible. I succeeded to a small extent, but in my heart I knew I was not cut out for the priesthood. I had many sessions with one of the priests stationed at the novitiate, and he was very understanding. He walked me through my emotional issues and doubts, but in the end looked me in the eye one day and said, matter-of-factly, "Jim, you don't have a vocation." His words did not excite me, but their sincerity told me he was totally correct in his assessment.

There was another factor, which I never mentioned to that priest and, to me, was a nudging of the Holy Spirit. Every night, without exception, I had a recurring dream that I was in a small boat, rowing furiously and knowing I had to reach the other shore – which I never did. At first, I did not put too much credence to the dream, but it kept nagging me every night, and for weeks I rowed that little boat without finding land.

To me, that dream had no logical basis. Situated in a heavily wooded part of New Jersey, there was no body of water of any kind for many miles. Little wonder that, for weeks on end, the nightly dream made no sense.

Then, and quite suddenly, the meaning of that dream slammed into me. I realized it was God's way of telling me I had to serve him in the world, but not in the priesthood. The Hudson River separated New York from New Jersey. It was that river on which I rowed in that recurring dream, because I was destined to leave new Jersey and discontinue my studies for the priesthood.

My decision had been made for me, but it did not make telling my parents I was leaving the novitiate any easier. They, and one of my aunts, were to visit a day or two after I figured out the meaning of the dream. With not a little reluctance, I dropped the bombshell on them. My mother almost went to pieces, and though my father was less emotional, I could see he was crushed. I had packed my personal items, and after the nice meal they brought for all the novices and priests, we piled into the car and headed back to Connecticut, with an uncomfortable and palpable silence heavily pervading the cramped interior of the car most of the way.

On an uncannily related note, that nightly rowing dream never entered my head again. God knew what he was doing, and I never looked back with any regret. I had reached the other shore.

To this day, I firmly believe the Holy Spirit was prodding me all the while. Little wonder he remains such a vital part of my life. I also feel quite strongly it is yet another reason God's existence makes no sense. He grants wishes in mysterious ways, sometimes, but his being is illogical in every human sense. That is why he is God. That is also why so many people cannot admit to his existence. He makes no human sense whatever.

If you can't believe in a God you can't understand, you are admitting his existence in an oblique way. You also are admitting to the greatest unknown that exists in the universe. The answer to that objection of not believing in a God you can't understand is this: If you did understand God, then he would not be God anymore.

God follows no rules; he doesn't have to do so. Because of granting us all free will, God never forces us to love him, either. We are perfectly free to accept or reject his existence. After all, in human terms he cannot exist. Yet, no one has ever explained how the vast, seemingly endless universe is out there for all of us to see. One friend of mine, a nonbeliever, said something like the Big Bang Theory created everything here and throughout infinity. He said it was a force. Aha! Another truth-sayer, but one not realizing he was admitting the existence of a higher power. Indeed, a "force" created everything. We who believe call that force God.

God was, is, and always will be, but never understood by anyone. Thank heaven for that!

Chapter 10:
Marriage, Children, and Tragedy

"I take you to be my lawfully wedded (wife/husband), to have and to hold from this day forward, for better or for worse, for richer, for poorer, to love and to cherish; from this day forward until death do us part."

(the wedding vows Dottie and I both recited on August 9, 1969)

Long before I met Dorothy de Gross, the woman who was to become my wife, my seminary days ended and I returned to college, where I received a bachelor's degree in English, and landed a job as a copywriter in a manufacturing company. At the same time, I lost my exemption to the military draft, which was in effect in the early 1960s.

Being an honest sort, I did not lie and say I was going to graduate school. Those who were college students were exempt for as long as they were enrolled and could prove it. I notified that federal government agency that I was now a graduate and no longer a student. The draft notice arrived almost the day after I mailed my status to them. Not too anxious, were they!

Fortunately, I did not have to be drafted into the Army for two years. I was lucky to find an Army Reserve medical unit, and I served in it for the next six years. Summer camp every year was our only active-duty obligation. It was during those six years that I met Dorothy de Gross, the woman who was to become my wife.

There was somewhat of a down side to my Reserve days. In joining the Army, I fell back into secularism because of the constant cursing by most of the troops, as well as their heavy drinking. Attending parties, telling and listening to "dirty" jokes, cursing, and in general relapsing fully into worldly pleasures also was part of my landscape. No reason to say more; we all know what goes on outside church life.

When I met Dorothy, or "Dottie," as she liked to be called, both my tongue and my spiritual life improved dramatically. We became engaged about one year after getting together in married in her Catholic church on August 9, 1969. Her positive influence on me helped steer me on that narrow path Jesus mentioned. I could not have been happier.

My poor mother, still convinced I would return one day to the seminary, told Dottie I would never marry, because I was going to be a priest. Even two weeks before we exchanged wedding vows, she never ceased telling Dottie that only the priesthood, not marriage, was for me. Her fantasy, sad though it was, would never become reality. Looking back, I am surprised Dottie never threw in the towel and searched for someone else to marry. It was a stressful time for both of us.

Italian mothers and Jewish mothers graduate from the same school – the one that teaches them they know best what is good for their sons and they hover over them, hoping always to get their winning way. Both types of mothers really created the "helicopter parent" syndrome. It made my period of engagement to my then-fiancée rocky, to say the least.

The date of our tying the knot in itself is not unique or even unusual, but I had an opportunity to use it in an amusing way a few years after Dottie and I became husband and wife. One day at work, a young secretary in our office at the electric company approached me and asked, "When was Pearl Harbor Day?" Without hesitation I replied, "August 9, 1969." She thanked me and started to walk away but then, puzzled, said, "That doesn't sound right." I said, "Sure it is right. It's the day I got married." A little humor never hurts.

On a much more serious note, here is yet another example of how God watches over us. For more than five years, we tried to start a family, but nothing happened. My wife became depressed and moody, and frankly I felt helpless. Our marriage almost ended because of our not being able to produce a child. I am not being cavalier by saying "our". We both saw specialists and discovered I had a low sperm count and my wife, Dottie, had another issue that impeded her from getting pregnant.

It was far from the happiest of times in our married life, and a thick silence throughout the house occurred almost daily. She never directly accused me of being incapable of getting her pregnant, but neither did we have an active, intimate life. The door to that was mostly shut and locked. That did not help the health of our marriage, to say the least.

I was at a loss as to what to do, but one day, along came the Holy Spirit again and directed me to a Catholic adoption agency. It was close to Christmas, and the gloom in our house was deeper than ever. We decorated for Christmas, but the house seemed eerily vacant of any true joy and did not exude a festive aura.

So, one cold December day when I was off from work and Dottie was in the medical office that employed her, I drove to the local Catholic Family Services agency and spoke to a social worker there. She listened intently when I told her my wife and I wanted to adopt an infant. She took a lot of notes, and after the interview she said she would meet Dottie and me right after the New Year. She then said with a wide smile, "Tell your wife you both have received an early Christmas present." The process was under way.

Our initial contact with the social worker, Marie, right after the New Year had a lighter moment as we went through the interview. Marie revealed something of which I was totally unaware. When I had entered the agency that first day, I spoke to an elderly woman, a volunteer, at the front desk, and told her why I was there. She looked askance at me, but went to fetch the social worker. She had told the woman, "Marie, there's a man out in the lobby, and he wants to adopt a baby!" Maybe I should have made it clearer that my wife was part of the deal, as well. So much for not practicing what I preached to others about being good communicators!

We were accepted for the adoption process and welcomed our infant son into our home – perhaps appropriately – nine months later. Three years after that, we welcomed our infant daughter from the same agency. They became the ultimate joys of our life, and they still are in mine. Hard to believe those squalling little infants are now both in their 40's, have two children each, and are enjoying successful careers. God is good!

Thanks to the Holy Spirit, who led me to that adoption agency all those years ago, we went from morose to unlimited joy. God gave us two of the greatest gifts we could have ever received. Little wonder I have no doubts whatever about his existence. Things do not just happen; they are part of the Divine Plan. I believe in God, but not in coincidence. Everything that happens in life is part of that magnificent plan. That infernal rowboat dream reaped benefits of a different, but equally wonderful kind.

Then, there the opposite to happier times. The worst event to befall Dottie and me began several days before Christmas in the year 2012. It changed Dottie's life and mine forever. One morning I got out of bed, took my morning shower, and walked down the fourteen steps of our Colonial home. What I saw next stunned me to my soul. My wife was sitting between the foyer and the living room, almost in a trance. She had fallen down those fourteen steps and broken her neck.

God intervened and sent one of the best orthopedic surgeons in Connecticut to heal her two broken cervical vertebrae. She recovered fully, at least physically. But that was it. Emotionally, she was now devolving into another world of her own, and not a good one for her or our family. Slowly, she became a stranger and her once ebullient nature was replaced by nonsense gibberish and worse.

Even prior to that debilitating fall, I had noticed she wasn't acting herself. She was becoming moody, combative and very stubborn. The fall only exacerbated those moods, and having to spend six months in rehab made her mind sink further and further from reality. She could not even attend our son's wedding in June 2013.

What followed next was – I am being charitable – not a good patch. The Alzheimer's that had attacked her turned her into a screamer, comprising two constantly repeated "mantras": "I want to die!" and "I need help!" Sleep for me was virtually impossible, because the screaming went on day and night. Our forty-nine-year marriage was no more.

It was a terrible six years for everyone, and trying to calm my wife when she screamed long and loud continually was an almost impossible task. It was quite a thrill during the night when I heard, "I need help!" or, "I want to die!" She screamed those meaningless pleas all day, as well.

In fact, on a warm spring day my daughter opened the sliding glass door in the living room, so my wife could have some fresh air. No sooner did she do so when the screaming started. About a half-hour later, the doorbell rang and I met two local police officers face-to-face. A neighbor had heard the scream for help and called them. Fortunately, Dottie started that same yell while they were there and were satisfied I was not abusing her.

That neighbor's action did not upset me at all. In fact, I was warmed by the knowledge he or she cared to call the police. Elder abuse is, unfortunately, a major problem. Thank goodness there are some wonderful and caring people out there.

My wife's six-year struggle with Alzheimer's was certainly no picnic, but it bonded our little family more tightly. During Dottie's debilitating illness my son, Jim, phoned regularly, and visited as often as he and his wife could. (They lived more than 50 miles from our town.) Our daughter, Jennifer, was an invaluable caregiver when our paid pert-time caregiver was not attending Dottie. I would have been a wreck without her caring help and her comforting me on the many down days.

What I am going to say here is neither bragging nor an attempt to have you see me as a model of marital heroism. A few people, perhaps meaning well, knew of the extreme difficulty my family and I were undergoing as my wife descended rapidly into the pit of that terrible disease. They asked me if I would consider putting her into a home for better care, and to give me a break. To all of them, my answer was an unwavering, "We married for better or for worse, and this is worse."

One friend even wondered aloud if I cheated on her, since she was no longer a wife in the usual sense. I simply reminded that person that I was a Catholic under marriage vows and adultery was not on my bucket list. He was shocked but also did not pursue the matter further.

After more than six years of her slide into mental oblivion, God called her home on September 27, 2018. She is with the Lord forever now, but not forgotten. I have retained the memories of our better years. I know she is in heaven; her suffering on Earth, which was a personal purgatory, ended forever. She is enjoying eternal happiness in the Lord's presence and in the bosom of our Blessed Mother.

God did not cause my wife's disease; nature did. She suffered for those long years, but I am convinced God permitted it to increase joy on the day he sent angels to bring her to him. It never entered my mind to blame God for all the trials we both underwent. Faith and as much understanding as I could conjure up told me the Creator of everything tests us here on Earth in preparation for eternal life.

No one enjoys physical or mental suffering. I have yet to meet the person who says, "I wish God would cause me severe pain that never ends." In life, we play the cards we are dealt. Sometimes the hand is a royal flush; other times, it is a total bust. God's love is the only constant, and it never ends. I fully accept his will, even though tragedies intervene. Life was never meant to be a bed of roses.

Chapter 11:
"It's All God's Fault!" (Wanna Bet?)

*"God does nothing to harm someone. It is the devil who does
these things to turn one against God."*

(Anonymous)

I concluded the preceding chapter by saying God did not cause
my wife's suffering; nature did. Over the years, I have heard so
many blame God for some serious issue in their lives. We have all
heard the following, or similar lines: "Why did God let this
happen?" "Why did God let my husband die?" "Why didn't God
answer my prayers?" "What happened to me was all his fault."

One of the quirkiest statements came from the mouth of my
mother's friend one day many years ago, when she and my mother
were discussing a terrible auto accident that took several lives.
Her friend said, "God made a big sin."

Last I knew, God does not make any sins; only humans can do
that. By the way, she was the same person who said, about a year
before men flew to the moon, "They will never go to the moon,
because that is where God is." Forgive me for not agreeing. I
believe God is in a place much more welcoming than the rocks
and craters of the moon. Neil Armstrong, the first man to walk on
the moon, did not indicate any sighting of the Father, either. What
better non-witness than that?

The hard truth is, we make our own decisions, for better or
worse. If something, such as an auto accident, house fire, or
another serious event comes our way, God did not direct those

things to happen. They occur for various reasons, from carelessness on our part to faulty wiring, driving recklessly, and so forth.

Of course, we are not always the cause of our dilemmas, but neither is God. It is the easiest thing in the world to put the onus on the Creator, especially when multiple deaths happen, such as mass shootings, multi-fatal accidents, or in parents dying young and leaving a virtually helpless family. Horrible events, such as the Holocaust, Joseph Stalin's executing nine million of his own people, and the unspeakable events of September 11, 2001, when almost three thousand people were killed as terrorists guided hijacked planes into the Twin Towers in Manhattan do make us wonder why God did not intervene.

All of us, including me, have asked the same question as to why God allows such terrible tragedies to take place. Why, indeed, did God let them happen? The answer is we all have free will. Adolph Hitler did not have to try to kill Jews, and Joseph Stalin did not need to outdo Hitler and slaughter even more people – mostly his own citizens. But they both were ruthless in their eliminating millions of innocent people.

Stalin was not only a senseless, mindless murderer, but was also possessed with a dark cynicism. Though he did not usually grant interviews to outsiders, he invited writer George Bernard Shaw and Mary Astor, both of Great Britain, to interview him, in 1931. Astor was noted for being quite pointed in her interviewing technique. She looked Stalin in the eye and asked darkly, "When are you going to stop killing people?" Stalin, unruffled, replied, "When it is no longer necessary. Soon, I hope."

"Soon" never came. People were executed, sent to freezing labor camps, starved, and killed in other ways. So, where was God in all this? In heaven, of course, overseeing all his sons and daughters here, and loving them all. Why did he not stop the slaughters, wars and other horrible atrocities? Because from Adam and Eve, the Creator gave every human being the gift of free will.

Unfortunately, some abuse it to a horrific degree, with the result in death or punishment of countless numbers of innocent people. God did not put the sick idea of killing people into Hitler's or Stalin's heads; they did their own devastating thinking and committed unspeakable crimes against those whom they did not want around anymore.

When God created men and women, he gave them a special power and ability to think independently, make their own paths in life, and did not interfere. Nor does he do so today.

Yes, there are times, especially in tragic events, that test our belief. A child contracts a fatal disease and passes away at a young age. Husband and wife find they have irreconcilable differences and divorce. Gambling, drugs or drinking drive a wedge among family members or friends. In my lifetime, I have seen or read about such countless and horrible events and how they tear the fabric of lives into shreds.

Why, many people ask, did that person die so young? Why did God allow mass shootings to cut lives short? Why did he cause an accident that left that young woman paralyzed? People ask those and many other questions, and too often God gets the blame. "Why did God let this happen?" The answer, and I am not being flippant or dismissive, is he did not. No question some events are totally beyond our control, especially lingering diseases, or sudden traumatic events. No matter the root cause, God is never responsible for those tragedies occurring.

The fact is, God made us imperfect beings, in mind and body. We are all born, we live a certain number of years, and then we die. Simple on the surface, yet immensely complicated. Whether or not we create our own problems or tragedy occurs without our doing anything wrong, God is not the one to blame.

We all feel the pain when a spouse or child dies young, when we lose our job, when we take a different route to work and get into an accident. We cannot blame God, and we cannot blame ourselves, either. I would never say that God planned those negatives for us. Yes, he sees all we are and all we do, but he is all-loving and all-forgiving. We must come to the realization that life on Earth is never perfect. Bad things happen to everyone, but the Almighty does not cause any of it.

Look, I am no different from anyone else in wondering why we feel God allows bad things to happen. For many years, I went with the tide of questioning, falling in with the "why" crowd. Though God's will for all human beings is one of love and – assuming we lead good lives – of eternal salvation.

As I grew older and walked inexorably to retirement age and beyond, I came to realize that no matter how horrible the things that happen to us, there is a rebirth to a place with no suffering, tears, or heartbreak. There, we will see the Creator face-to-face and have nothing but unending happiness. Did my thinking result in total understanding? Hardly. No matter what happens, and how much tragedy hits, I know God is there to comfort me – always.

Chapter 12:
Seeking and Finding Comfort

*"For if we believe that Jesus died and rose, and so too will God,
through Jesus, bring with him those who
have fallen asleep."*

(1 Thessalonians 4:14)

Death is the ultimate finale of life. Admittedly, it is not the brightest statement I have ever made, but there is no question whatever, that at some point our existence comes to an end here on Earth. What lies ahead after that? For those who do not believe in an afterlife, they claim we just stop breathing and our existence is simply ended. Others say you are granted a new life and return in a different form of life.

Believers in eternal life maintain we die but are raised by God to eternal joy, where no illness, anger, hatred, or any other of earthly life's woes are to be found. Happiness abounds without end in God's kingdom.

My vote is for those who believe in a single life journey that ends here, but continues endlessly in what is called heaven. Heck, Jesus himself used the expression, "kingdom of heaven", throughout the gospels, especially when introducing a parable. Never try to contradict the Lord. How terrible when some nonbelievers maintain that nothing lies in a future life. Die and goodbye. Noting is beyond this life.

Au contraire! Proof to the contrary came from the preaching of Jesus himself. He promised eternal salvation to all who believe in him. Great, but we need to proceed with a bit of caution here. As discussed in an earlier chapter, believing is not enough, though is the bedrock upon which our faith develops and grows without stopping. Leading a sinless life as possible and rejecting vices – those insidious soul-killers – keep us in God's grace and set us on the wonderful path to one day reap the incredible and never-ending rewards that await us.

In Luke (13:33-30), the Lord made it quite clear that personal salvation must be attained through good living and good works. As he walked through towns on his way to Jerusalem, someone following him asked, "Lord, will only a few people be saved?"

He answered the one posing the question with a metaphorical reference:

"Strive to enter through the narrow gate, for many, I tell you, will attempt to enter but will not be strong enough. After the master of the house has arisen and locked the door, then will you stand outside knocking and saying, 'Lord, open the door for us. He will say to you in reply, 'I do not know where you are from.' And you will say, 'We ate and drank in your company and you taught in our streets.' Then he will say to you, 'I do not know where you are from. Depart from me, all you evildoers!' And there will be wailing and grinding of teeth.''

To me, the Lord's cautionary words mean the "narrow gate" is achieved by excluding all negative and sinful elements from my life. The road to destruction is wide, but the path to eternal life is much narrower. Of course, it isn't easy! Jesus never said it would be. How many hundreds or more times in my years, even now in my eighth decade of life, have I had immoral desires, or cave in to siren other calls to give into pleasurable, but sinful behavior?

That narrow path will widen to the road to destruction if I fall into that soul-killing mentality.

When God calls me for judgment, the words from Matthew's gospel as to that God will say to me are in my consciousness daily. "Well done, good and faithful servant..." or, "Depart from me, you accursed..." The first is the statement I hope to hear; the second means consignment to hell with no chance for parole. If that isn't the most frightening alternative, I don't know what is.

No perfect human beings, except for Jesus and Mary, have ever walked the earth. The good news is, God fully understands our flaws, warts and imperfections. All he asks is that we try and do so every say. Few of us will experience visions, be awarded the stigmata, or be able to levitate or bilocate. That does not make us any less faithful than those wonderful saints who experienced such gifts. God loves all, regardless of status in life. All he asks that we love him, in return. It does not cost a single cent to be in his grace.

A Final Word

There is much more I could say about my faith and what it means to me, though I feel I have yammered at it long enough. Faith is not earned; it is the most incredible gift from the Creator, the Person we call God. I make zero claims to be sinless, perfect in my prayer life, or saint material. Daily, I pray that God will treat me with kindness, wipe away all my sins, and bring me to himself when this life ends. That also means leading as holy a life as possible, and not deliberately falling from grace for some defiant and seriously amoral act.

If God indeed holds all my past sins, especially mortal ones, against me, I am doomed eternally. The fact is, however, I believe in an all-forgiving God, one who, while not at all appreciative of my straying into sin, especially in my younger days, will nonetheless know that I confessed all those sins, and so I pray he will admit me to heaven for trying to never offend him again after seeking Jesus' forgiveness through the aegis of the priest.

I firmly believe God is not only all-forgiving, but also takes into consideration our frail human nature. I also am totally convinced that he created the world and gave us all the free will to love or not love him, to do his will, or not even acknowledge his existence. Thus, this earthly life is a trial period, in which we are born into the world and make choices that will either secure his everlasting love, or cause his condemnation.

The key to the narrow path, about which Jesus spoke in Luke's gospel, is there for every human being. Yes, the wide path, the all-too-tempting call of the world's vices, devious behavior, drugs, wanton sex and so many other anti-faith actions can ruin a soul forever.

Instead, I chose another daily route, one that involves daily Mass, numerous prayers, including the Little Office of the Blessed Mother, being generous to less-fortunate people, and in general trying to be a supportive friend to one and all. While those spiritual activities do not automatically qualify me for sainthood, they keep me anchored on the narrower path that leads to eternal life.

The martyrs are especially wonderful role models for everyone, being so steadfast and in some instances even joyous, knowing God's eternal home was worth the torture, excruciating as it was for some of them, because they knew, through their unbending faith, that their physical suffering would be gone forever when God took their immortal souls to himself.

All saints, martyrs or not, who led lives of incredible prayer practices, fasting, helping others, or in so many other virtuous ways, are equally to be emulated and cherished. Following their examples is sure to enhance our own faith lives exponentially.

You probably will be surprised at the following statement, but it is a fact we are all martyrs, though not in the sense of being physically tortured. Resisting sin on a daily basis, being charitable and giving to others, and setting an example of our Christian commitment is not always easy. When we shun the temptations with which we deal every day, when we resolutely follow all the precepts of the Church and turn from all evil, we are modern-day martyrs. Perhaps more important, we also are role models for all others whose lives we touch.

No, the road to salvation is not easily attainable. Nothing worth attaining is easy, and staying in God's grace is the most difficult of all. The good news is, it can be done in so many ways – attending Mass more frequently, saying the rosary, Divine Chaplet and other supplications every day, and adding to church rites, such as First Friday Adoration or other devotional exercises.

I absolutely guarantee doing that will not only cleanse your mind and soul, but also will open your spiritual eyes to the true glory of the Holy Trinity, our Blessed Mother, and all the saints to whom we pray. Further, a more intense spiritual life will help you treat others with love and respect. A sort of bonus is that when you do all this, you will see you have never felt better about yourself.

Remember, too, that humor is often something that suppresses our temptations. And since I sprinkled humor throughout this work, knowing God gave us a sense of humor for a good reason, I want to close with a funny story I heard at Mass one Sunday, which made the congregation laugh loudly.

A 12-year-old boy was disrespectful to his parents and others, and his mother and father were worn to a frazzle after trying all they could to alter his behavior. They thought their parish priest could help, and drove the boy to the rectory to see him.

He went into the rectory and the priest greeted him warmly in his office. After a bit of informal talk the priest said to the boy, "God is in heaven, and sees everything you do." He then instructed the boy about God's presence, occasionally saying, "Remember, God is in heaven and sees everything you do."

After about an hour, the priest asked the boy, "Now, where is God?" The kid just stared at him. So, the priest repeated, "Where is God?" Same silence. Frustrated, the priest pounded his fist on the desk and said loudly, "Where is God?" The boy jumped up and ran back to his parents' car, crying his eyes out. His mother, startled, asked, "What happened?" The boy replied, trembling, "God is missing, and the priest is blaming me!"

May God never be absent from your life, and may his everlasting grace be with you always.

God makes absolutely no sense, and that is why we believe.

Addendum

Daily Prayers that Bring Us Closer to God

"Lord, teach us to pray, just as John taught his disciples."
(Luke 11:2)

Yes, our prayer life is important, and the well-known Catholic prayers with which we are all familiar form the base of our spiritual portion of the day. That said, the greatest thing about praying is that our talking to God, the Blessed Mother, or the saints does not have to always be structured. Rather, whatever we say, ask for, or give thanks can be spontaneous. Those supplications are no less sincere than any structured prayers.

Another wonderful thing about praying is there is no limit. You can offer brief morning and nighttime prayers, or get very deeply into them by reciting as many pleas, thank-you expressions or anything else. God listens to all and loves all who beseech him.

My everyday prayer routine begins upon awakening, when I thank God for the gifts of life and faith. That is followed by prayers to the Father, Son, Holy Spirit, Blessed Mother, and special (to me) saints, as well as both to and for deceased members of my family, my wife's family, and those friends who also have been called home. Then, I pray five decades of the Rosary for different intentions – the same ones every day. The Divine Chaplet, a plea for peace in our nation to Saint Faustina, is the final prayer.

By the way, I offer these daily prayers while still in bed. Someone once told me that is "cheating", but I like to think God does not care if we are kneeling, standing, or lying under a blanket. He listens to everything we say, regardless.

Each morning, except for Sundays, we have a little group that gathers at my parish, Saint Peter the Apostle in Naples a half-hour before Mass time, for the recitation of the rosary. I am honored to offer one of the five decades every day, except Sunday, when I recite it privately, also prior to Mass.

All my daily prayers, collectively, take about an hour of my time. Some are the familiar structured prayers, some are spontaneous and not-so-structured. As the bumper sticker I saw some years ago read, "Pray always, pray all ways." Great advice!

Following are prayer suggestions, which you can follow or, as I said, pray in your own special way. God always listens and smiles on you.

A Prayer Sampling

Praying to God is as old as humanity itself. Even a casual thumbing through the books of the Old Testament is replete with numerous examples of pleas, thanksgiving, remorse, and so forth.

Then, a man named Jesus came along and imparted to his disciples a prayer which, more than two thousand years later, remains as the core supplication of every Christian's prayer life. Jesus presented his disciples with the beloved prayer that will be with us forever.

The disciples of Jesus, having observed him going off from them to pray privately to the Father, had not yet fully immersed themselves in any prayer methods. One (unnamed) disciple plaintively made a plea to the Lord, saying, *"Lord, teach us to pray, just as John taught his disciples.* " (Luke 11:1) None of the Twelve knew what Jesus would say in reply, and they were probably both startled and pleased by the simple prayer Jesus gave to them, the Our Father. (Note: In Matthew 9-13, Jesus initiated that prayer during the Sermon on the Mount, and it is the version we use today.)

When we pray to the Father, Son, Holy Spirit and Blessed Mother, or to our favorite saints, we need not let thousands of words flow from our lips. It is quality of sincerity, not quantity of words that pleases God the most. As Jesus instructed us during the Sermon on the Mount (Matthew 6:6-8):

"...when you pray, go to your inner room, close the door, and pray to your Father in secret. And you Father who sees you in secret will repay you. In praying, do not babble like the pagans, who think they will be heard because of their many words. Do not be like them. Your Father knows what you need before you ask him."

No argument there; you could not have a better source for that great advice than from the Son of God himself.

Unlike going to the dentist, increasing your daily prayer routine is not at all like pulling teeth. Think about how much time you actually spend with those prayers, and you will see they do not at all interfere with your routine one iota.

Best of all, you don't have to be in church; you can pray just as easily in your home, while in your car, even at work when on break. God listens and hears all your prayers. He is, of course, all-knowing.

What prayers or supplications can be part of your morning, evening or whenever you choose to talk with God? Here are a few for your consideration, but do keep in mind there are no limits. You can "invent" pleas to God in your own words; and not just use the common prayers. It is also spiritually uplifting to also recite the prayers so many of us learned from childhood:

The Our Father

Hail Mary

the Memorare ("Remember, O Gracious Virgin Mary…")

Glory be to the Father, Son and Holy Spirit

Apostles Creed

Daily Rosary (the Mysteries vary daily, but pamphlets explaining when to say them are always at your church.

The Divine Chaplet

The Chaplet of Divine Mercy is a popular devotion, said on rosary beads, which was promoted by Saint Maria Faustina Kowolska, a Polish nun who lived from 1905-1938. Saint Faustina received the prayers for this devotion in a vision. It takes only a few minutes to offer your request by reciting this beautiful devotion. There are optional prayers that accompany this chaplet, so it is best to go online and see which version you wish to use. The chaplet itself begins with the Apostles Creed, followed by one Our Father, one Hail Mary, and the Glory be. Then, the five decades are recited as follows:

(On the bead usually when the Our Father is said) "Eternal Father, I offer you the Body and Blood, Soul and Divinity, of your beloved Son in reparation for my sins and those of the whole world." The ten (usually) Hail Mary beads are replaced with, "For the sake of his sorrowful passion, have mercy on us and on the whole world." After the fifth decade is completed, you say, three times, "Holy God, Holy Mighty One, Holy Immortal One, have mercy on us and on the whole world." I always offer the Chaplets for world and family peace and for special intentions.

Amen

Yes, with that word I conclude this journey and hope you enjoyed reading it. But there is more. We all use the word, "amen," mostly in prayer, but also in secular conversations. For example, if you or I say something with which the other person agrees, he or she is likely to say, "Amen, to that," or something similar. "Amen" also sometimes is a one-word answer to a concluding statement or other bit of conversation.

Of all the words we say in any prayer, "amen" is always literally the last word. "Amen" is so inured into our consciousness that it is even more automatic than reciting the common prayers themselves. In Christianity, it means, "So be it," or a similar designation. So, following a prayer, it is our affirmation that we accept the Our Father, Hail Mary, Creed or any other recited prayer unequivocally as part of our faith belief.

The word itself is thousands of years old, first appearing in the Old Testament in the Book of Numbers (5:22): "*May this water, then, that brings a curse, enter your body to make your belly swell and your thighs waste away! And the woman shall say, 'Amen, amen.'*"

You also will find the word in Psalm 41:13, 1 Chronicles 13:36, Nehemiah 5:13 and hundreds of times in the New Testament, especially the gospels. Jesus used a double "amen" in John's gospel, single in the others.

You can find a great article regarding "amen" in the following website: pray.com/articles/amen-meaning-origin-and-why-we-say-it

Amen again!

The Holy Spirit's Beautiful Presence from the prophets to Revelation (complete list)

Matthew 1:18 This is how the birth of Jesus the Messiah came about: His mother Mary was pledged to be married to Joseph, but before they came together, she was found to be pregnant through the **Holy Spirit,**

Matthew 1:20 But after he had considered this, an angel of the Lord appeared to him in a dream and said, "Joseph son of David, do not be afraid to take Mary home as your wife, because what is conceived in her is from the **Holy Spirit.**"

Matthew 3:11 "I baptize you with water for repentance. But after me comes one who is more powerful than I, whose sandals I am not worthy to carry. He will baptize you with the **Holy Spirit** and fire."

Matthew 12:32 "Anyone who speaks a word against the Son of Man will be forgiven, but anyone who speaks against the **Holy Spirit** will not be forgiven, either in this age or in the age to come."

Matthew 28:19 "Therefore go and make disciples of all nations, baptizing them in the name of the Father and of the Son and of the **Holy Spirit,**"

Mark 1:8 "I baptize you with water, but he will baptize you with the **Holy Spirit.**"

Mark 3:29 "but whoever blasphemes against the **Holy Spirit** will never be forgiven; they are guilty of an eternal sin."

Mark 12:36 David himself, speaking by the **Holy Spirit**, declared: "'The Lord said to my Lord: "Sit at my right hand until I put your enemies under your feet."'"

Mark 13:11 "Whenever you are arrested and brought to trial, do not worry beforehand about what to say. Just say whatever is given you at the time, for it is not you speaking, but the **Holy Spirit**."

Luke 1:15 "for he will be great in the sight of the Lord. He is never to take wine or other fermented drink, and he will be filled with the **Holy Spirit** even before he is born."

Luke 1:35 The angel answered, "The **Holy Spirit** will come on you, and the power of the Most High will overshadow you. So the **holy** one to be born will be called the Son of God."

Luke 1:41 When Elizabeth heard Mary's greeting, the baby leaped in her womb, and Elizabeth was filled with the **Holy Spirit**.

Luke 1:67 His father Zechariah was filled with the **Holy Spirit** and prophesied:

Luke 2:25 Now there was a man in Jerusalem called Simeon, who was righteous and devout. He was waiting for the consolation of Israel, and the **Holy Spirit** was on him.

Luke 2:26 It had been revealed to him by the **Holy Spirit** that he would not die before he had seen the Lord's Messiah

Luke 3:16 John answered them all, "I baptize you with water. But one who is more powerful than I will come, the straps of whose sandals I am not worthy to untie. He will baptize you with the **Holy Spirit** and fire."

Luke 3:22 and the **Holy Spirit** descended on him in bodily form like a dove. And a voice came from heaven: "You are my Son, whom I love; with you I am well pleased."

Luke 4:1 Jesus, full of the **Holy Spirit**, left the Jordan and was led by the **Spirit** into the wilderness,

Luke 10:21 At that time Jesus, full of joy through the **Holy Spirit**, said, "I praise you, Father, Lord of heaven and earth, because you have hidden these things from the wise and learned, and revealed them to little children. Yes, Father, for this is what you were pleased to do."

Luke 11:13 "If you then, though you are evil, know how to give good gifts to your children, how much more will your Father in heaven give the **Holy Spirit** to those who ask him!"

Luke 12:10 "And everyone who speaks a word against the Son of Man will be forgiven, but anyone who blasphemes against the **Holy Spirit** will not be forgiven."

Luke 12:12 "for the **Holy Spirit** will teach you at that time what you should say."

John 1:33 "And I myself did not know him, but the one who sent me to baptize with water told me, 'The man on whom you see the **Spirit** come down and remain is the one who will baptize with the **Holy Spirit**.'"

John 14:15 "If you love me, keep my commands. And I will ask the Father, and he will give you another Advocate to be with you always, the Spirit of truth, which the world cannot accept, because it neither sees nor knows it. But you know it, because it remains with you, and will be in you."

<u>John 14:26</u> "But the Advocate, the **Holy Spirit**, whom the Father will send in my name, will teach you all things and will remind you of everything I have said to you."

<u>John 15:26</u> "When the Advocate comes, whom I will send to you from the Father—the **Spirit** of truth who goes out from the Father—he will testify about me."

<u>John 20:22</u> And with that he breathed on them and said, "Receive the **Holy Spirit**."

<u>Acts 1:2</u> until the day he was taken up to heaven, after giving instructions through the **Holy Spirit** to the apostles he had chosen.

<u>Acts 1:5</u> "For John baptized with water, but in a few days you will be baptized with the **Holy Spirit**."

<u>Acts 1:8</u> "But you will receive power when the **Holy Spirit** comes on you; and you will be my witnesses in Jerusalem, and in all Judea and Samaria, and to the ends of the earth."

<u>Acts 1:16</u> and said, "Brothers and sisters, the Scripture had to be fulfilled in which the **Holy Spirit** spoke long ago through David concerning Judas, who served as guide for those who arrested Jesus."

<u>Acts 2:1</u> When the day of Pentecost came, they were all together in one place.

<u>Acts 2:4</u> All of them were filled with the **Holy Spirit** and began to speak in other tongues as the **Spirit** enabled them.

Acts 2:33 "Exalted to the right hand of God, he has received from the Father the promised **Holy Spirit** and has poured out what you now see and hear."

Acts 2:38 Peter replied, "Repent and be baptized, every one of you, in the name of Jesus Christ for the forgiveness of your sins. And you will receive the gift of the **Holy Spirit**."

Acts 4:8 Then Peter, filled with the **Holy Spirit**, said to them: "Rulers and elders of the people!"

Acts 4:25 "You spoke by the **Holy Spirit** through the mouth of your servant, our father David: "'Why do the nations rage and the peoples plot in vain?"

Acts 4:31 After they prayed, the place where they were meeting was shaken. And they were all filled with the **Holy Spirit** and spoke the word of God boldly.

Acts 5:3 Then Peter said, "Ananias, how is it that Satan has so filled your heart that you have lied to the **Holy Spirit** and have kept for yourself some of the money you received for the land?"

Acts 5:32 "We are witnesses of these things, and so is the **Holy Spirit**, whom God has given to those who obey him."

Acts 6:5 This proposal pleased the whole group. They chose Stephen, a man full of faith and of the **Holy Spirit**; also Philip, Procorus, Nicanor, Timon, Parmenas, and Nicolas from Antioch, a convert to Judaism.

Acts 7:51 "You stiff-necked people! Your hearts and ears are still uncircumcised. You are just like your ancestors: You always resist the **Holy Spirit**!"

<u>Acts 7:55</u> But Stephen, full of the **Holy Spirit**, looked up to heaven and saw the glory of God, and Jesus standing at the right hand of God.

<u>Acts 8:15</u> When they arrived, they prayed for the new believers there that they might receive the **Holy Spirit**,

<u>Acts 8:16</u> because the **Holy Spirit** had not yet come on any of them; they had simply been baptized in the name of the Lord Jesus.

<u>Acts 8:17</u> Then Peter and John placed their hands on them, and they received the **Holy Spirit**.

<u>Acts 8:19</u> and said, "Give me also this ability so that everyone on whom I lay my hands may receive the **Holy Spirit**."

<u>Acts 9:17</u> Then Ananias went to the house and entered it. Placing his hands on Saul, he said, "Brother Saul, the Lord—Jesus, who appeared to you on the road as you were coming here—has sent me so that you may see again and be filled with the **Holy Spirit**."

<u>Acts 9:31</u> Then the church throughout Judea, Galilee and Samaria enjoyed a time of peace and was strengthened. Living in the fear of the Lord and encouraged by the **Holy Spirit**, it increased in numbers.

<u>Acts 10:38</u> how God anointed Jesus of Nazareth with the **Holy Spirit** and power, and how he went around doing good and healing all who were under the power of the devil, because God was with him.

<u>Acts 10:44</u> While Peter was still speaking these words, the **Holy Spirit** came on all who heard the message.

<u>Acts 10:45</u> The circumcised believers who had come with Peter were astonished that the gift of the **Holy Spirit** had been poured out even on Gentiles.

<u>Acts 10:47</u> "Surely no one can stand in the way of their being baptized with water. They have received the **Holy Spirit** just as we have."

<u>Acts 11:15</u> "As I began to speak, the **Holy Spirit** came on them as he had come on us at the beginning.

<u>Acts 11:16</u> Then I remembered what the Lord had said: 'John baptized with water, but you will be baptized with the **Holy Spirit**.'

<u>Acts 11:24</u> He was a good man, full of the **Holy Spirit** and faith, and a great number of people were brought to the Lord.

<u>Acts 13:2</u> While they were worshiping the Lord and fasting, the **Holy Spirit** said, "Set apart for me Barnabas and Saul for the work to which I have called them."

<u>Acts 13:4</u> The two of them, sent on their way by the **Holy Spirit**, went down to Seleucia and sailed from there to Cyprus.

<u>Acts 13:9</u> Then Saul, who was also called Paul, filled with the **Holy Spirit**, looked straight a Elymas and said,

<u>Acts 13:52</u> And the disciples were filled with joy and with the **Holy Spirit**.

<u>Acts 15:8</u> God, who knows the heart, showed that he accepted them by giving the **Holy Spirit** to them, just as he did to us.

<u>Acts 15:28</u> "It seemed good to the **Holy Spirit** and to us not to burden you with anything beyond the following requirements…"

<u>Acts 16:6</u> Paul and his companions traveled throughout the region of Phrygia and Galatia, having been kept by the **Holy Spirit** from preaching the word in the province of Asia.

<u>Acts 19:2</u> and asked them, "Did you receive the **Holy Spirit** when you believed?" They answered, "No, we have not even heard that there is a **Holy Spirit**."

<u>Acts 19:6</u> When Paul placed his hands on them, the **Holy Spirit** came on them, and they spoke in tongues and prophesied.

<u>Acts 20:23</u> "I only know that in every city the **Holy Spirit** warns me that prison and hardships are facing me."

<u>Acts 20:28</u>" Keep watch over yourselves and all the flock of which the **Holy Spirit** has made you overseers. Be shepherds of the church of God, which he bought with his own blood."

<u>Acts 21:11</u> Coming over to us, he took Paul's belt, tied his own hands and feet with it and said, "The **Holy Spirit** says, 'In this way the Jewish leaders in Jerusalem will bind the owner of this belt and will hand him over to the Gentiles.'"

<u>Acts 28:25</u> They disagreed among themselves and began to leave after Paul had made this final statement: "The **Holy Spirit** spoke the truth to your ancestors when he said through Isaiah the prophet…"

<u>Romans 5:5</u> "And hope does not put us to shame, because God's love has been poured out into our hearts through the **Holy Spirit**, who has been given to us."

<u>Romans 9:1</u> "I speak the truth in Christ—I am not lying, my conscience confirms it through the **Holy Spirit**"

<u>Romans 14:17</u> "For the kingdom of God is not a matter of eating and drinking, but of righteousness, peace and joy in the **Holy Spirit**,"

<u>Romans 15:13</u> "May the God of hope fill you with all joy and peace as you trust in him, so that you may overflow with hope by the power of the **Holy Spirit**."

<u>Romans 15:16</u> "to be a minister of Christ Jesus to the Gentiles. He gave me the priestly duty of proclaiming the gospel of God, so that the Gentiles might become an offering acceptable to God, sanctified by the **Holy Spirit**."

<u>1 Corinthians 6:19</u> "Do you not know that your bodies are temples of the **Holy Spirit**, who is in you, whom you have received from God? You are not your own;"

<u>1 Corinthians 12:3</u> "Therefore I want you to know that no one who is speaking by the **Spirit** of God says, "Jesus be cursed," and no one can say, "Jesus is Lord," except by the **Holy Spirit**."

<u>2 Corinthians 6:6</u> "in purity, understanding, patience and kindness; in the **Holy Spirit** and in sincere love;"

<u>2 Corinthians 13:14</u> "May the grace of the Lord Jesus Christ, and the love of God, and the fellowship of the **Holy Spirit** be with you all."

<u>Ephesians 1:13</u> "And you also were included in Christ when you heard the message of truth, the gospel of your salvation. When you believed, you were marked in him with a seal, the promised **Holy Spirit**,"

Ephesians 3:5 "which was not made known to people in other generations as it has now been revealed by the **Spirit** to God's **holy** apostles and prophets."

Ephesians 4:30 "And do not grieve the **Holy Spirit** of God, with whom you were sealed for the day of redemption."

1 Thessalonians 1:5 "because our gospel came to you not simply with words but also with power, with the **Holy Spirit** and deep conviction. You know how we lived among you for your "sake.

1 Thessalonians 1:6 "You became imitators of us and of the Lord, for you welcomed the message in the midst of severe suffering with the joy given by the **Holy Spirit**."

1 Thessalonians 4:8 "Therefore, anyone who rejects this instruction does not reject a human being but God, the very God who gives you his **Holy Spirit**."

2 Timothy 1:14 "Guard the good deposit that was entrusted to you—guard it with the help of the **Holy Spirit** who lives in us."

Titus 3:5 "he saved us, not because of righteous things we had done, but because of his mercy. He saved us through the washing of rebirth and renewal by the **Holy Spirit**,"

Hebrews 2:4 God also testified to it by signs, wonders and various miracles, and by gifts of the **Holy Spirit** distributed according to his will.

Hebrews 3:7 So, as the **Holy Spirit** says: "Today, if you hear his voice,"

<u>Hebrews 6:4</u> "It is impossible for those who have once been enlightened, who have tasted the heavenly gift, who have shared in the **Holy Spirit**,"

<u>Hebrews 9:8</u> The **Holy Spirit** was showing by this that the way into the Most **Holy** Place had not yet been disclosed as long as the first tabernacle was still functioning.

<u>Hebrews 10:15</u> "The **Holy Spirit** also testifies to us about this. First he says:

<u>1 Peter 1:12</u> It was revealed to them that they were not serving themselves but you, when they spoke of the things that have now been told you by those who have preached the gospel to you by the **Holy Spirit** sent from heaven. Even angels long to look into these things."

<u>1 Peter 2:5</u> "you also, like living stones, are being built into a **spirit**ual house to be a **holy** priesthood, offering **spirit**ual sacrifices acceptable to God through Jesus Christ."

<u>2 Peter 1:21</u> For prophecy never had its origin in the human will, but prophets, though human, spoke from God as they were carried along by the **Holy Spirit**.

<u>Jude 1:20</u> "But you, dear friends, by building yourselves up in your most **holy** faith and praying in the **Holy Spirit**,"

<u>Revelation 21:10</u> "And he carried me away in the **Spirit** to a mountain great and high, and showed me the **Holy** City, Jerusalem, coming down out of heaven from God."

Works Cited

"Amen: Meaning, Origin and Why We Say It, online at: pray.com/articles/amen-meaning-origin-and-why-we-say-it

Arminjou, Father Charles, "The End of the Present World and the Mysteries of the Future Life" (1881 sermon)

de Caussade, Jean-Pierre, The Sacrament of the Present Moment (translated by Kitty Muggeridge). Harper San Francisco, 1989

archive.org/stream/EndOfThePresentWorldAndTArminjonFrCh arles_201903/End%20of%20the%20Present%20World

content.time.com/time/subscriber/article 1963

catholicnewsagency.com/column/51086/free-will-conscience-and-moral-choice-what-catholics-believe

contributions/catholic-doctrine-on-the-holy-trinityonline at cchaction.org

faculty.umb.edu/adam_beresford/courses/phil_100_11/reading_f ive_ways

find2god.com/confession

Hardon, John, S.J. catholiceducation.org/en/culture/catholic-contributions/catholic-doctrine-on-the-holy-trinity

inallthings.org/is-the-church-for-sinner-or-saints

inters.org/Vatican-Council-I-Dei-Filius

libquotes.com/stephen-hawking/quote

McKeow, Jonah, "Can't go to confession during coronavirus? Consider an 'act of perfect Contrition.' " Catholic News Agency magazine, March 27, 2020

New American Bible April 25, 1969

Niederauer, George, Most Reverend, Archbishop of San Francisco catholiceducation.org/en/culture/catholic (with permission)

search.yahoo.com/search;_ylt=AwrFebtoNAZjEc0CT4FXNyoA ;_ylu=Y29sbwNiZjEEcG9zAzIEdnRpZANMT0NVSTA1NENf MQRzZWMDcm (for Chapter 1 regarding God's existence)

Shirley, Steve, Steve, online at jesusalive.cc/miracles-Jesus-performed-on-sabbath

thecatholicthing.org/2016/06/22/who-is-god

catholiceducation.org/en/culture/catholic (with permission)

St Juliana of Norwich, qtd. From The Catholic Company online

the catholicthing.org

simplycatholic.com/age-of-reason

vaticannews.va/en/church/news/2018